Publisher Information

Published by

THE BIBLE FOR TODAY PRESS
900 Park Avenue
Collingswood, New Jersey 08108
U.S.A.

Pastor D. A. Waite, Th.D., Ph.D.

𝕭ible 𝕱or 𝕿oday 𝕭aptist 𝕮hurch
Church Phone: 856-854-4747
BFT Phone: 856-854-4452
Orders: 1-800-John 10:9
e-mail: BFT@BibleForToday.org
Website: www.BibleForToday.org
fax: 856-854-2464

We Use and Defend
The King James Bible

August, 2010
BFT 3473

Copyright, 2010
All Rights Reserved

ISBN #978-1-56848-070-1

Acknowledgments

I wish to acknowledge the assistance of the following people:

- **Yvonne Sanborn Waite**--my wife, for encouraging me to publish these questions and answers, for reading the manuscript carefully; and, for giving other helpful suggestions for the body of the book and for the cover.
- **Barbara Egan**--our **Bible For Today** secretary, for proofreading the manuscript; for suggesting various corrections; and for making valuable comments.
- **Julia Monaghan**–a faithful supporter of our **Bible For Today** ministry and an attender via the Internet of our **Bible For Today Baptist Church** services, who read the manuscript and gave helpful comments for correction.
- **Daniel S. Waite**--the Assistant to the **Bible For Today** Director, who kept my computer working properly; helped with the printing, and made important suggestions.
- **Dr. and Mrs. H. D. Williams**--friends in the **Bible For Today** and the **Dean Burgon Society** ministries, and attenders via the Internet of our **Bible For Today Baptist Church** services whose expertise in "print on demand" (POD) technology has made it possible for us to print this book in this manner, thus saving us hundreds of dollars in costs.

FOREWORD

- **Five Sections**. This is the second series of 200 questions that have been sent to me (## 201-400). I have answered them as simply and as clearly as possible. The answers to questions ##1-200 can be found in **BFT #3309 @ $12.00 + $7.00 S&H**.
- **Questions on New & Old Testaments**. In the order of the questions in this *Second 200 Questions Answered*, I have begun with questions dealing with the New Testament and its text. There were more questions on this theme than on any other. The next greatest number of questions were on the Old Testament and its text. For this reason, these questions are taken up next.
- **Miscellaneous Questions**. Some of the questions in this section include: (1) the authenticity of Mark 16:9-20; (2) would Dean Burgon revise the TR?; (3) a defense of 1 John 5:7-8; (4) females praying in mixed meetings; (5) Christ abolished Moses' law; (6) "corporate" election Explained; (7) the errors of Dan Wallace; (8) Acts 13:38 And "hyper-Calvinism"; (9) New Testament elders and house churches; (10) hyper-Calvinism and the decrees of God; (11) John MacArthur and the blood of Christ.
- **More Questions Answered**. (1) the value of the King James Bible; (2) inquiries about various modern Bible versions; (3) the position of women in the church; (4) reasons against women preachers; (5) the Biblical position on marriage, divorce, and remarriage; (6) Ephesians 2:8-9 explained clearly; (7) the author of the Pentateuch; (8) two Hebrew texts; (9) verses against drinking alcohol; (10) The KJB and derived inspiration; (11) Calvinism and the decrees of God. A 26-page INDEX is included in the back of the book to help you find material on many subjects.

Pastor D. A. Waite, Th.D., Ph.D.
Director of the **Bible For Today**, Incorporated, and
Pastor of the **Bible For Today Baptist Church**

Table of Contents

Publisher's Data i
Acknowledgments ii
Foreword iii
Table of Contents iv
Introductory Considerations 1
I.   Questions on the N.T. & Its Texts 3
II. Questions on the O.T. & Hebrew Subjects 37
III. Miscellaneous Questions   61
IV. Questions on the KJB & Various Bible Versions   107
V.   Questions on Marriage, Divorce, Remarriage   129
Index of Words and Phrases 141
About the Author 163
Order Blank Pages 165
Defined King James Bible Order Form 171

The Second 200 Questions Answered By Dr. D. A. Waite

Introductory Considerations

I don't know how many of you who are reading this book have already seen *THE FIRST 200 QUESTIONS ANSWERED*. If you have not seen it and want to look it over, you can order it as **BFT #3909 ($12.00 + $7.00 S&P)**. As I mentioned in that book, I was reluctant to write it. After it came out, for some reason, I began to work on *THE SECOND 200 QUESTIONS ANSWERED*. I changed my mind on writing question and answer books.

Though there might be questions in this second book that were included in the first book, they are asked by different people at different times. In fact, there are some questions in the present book that deal with the same subject, but were asked by different people. For this reason I have included the subject more than once. As you will note, I have included 26 pages of an *Index of Words and Phrases* found in this book. This will help you find various topics of interest.

CHAPTER I
QUESTIONS ON THE N.T. AND ITS TEXTS

"Faults" And "Sins"
QUESTION #201
Should it be *"faults"* or *"sins"* in James 5:16? What about 1 Peter 2:20?
ANSWER #201
In James 5:16, the critical text uses HARMARTIA or *"sins"* and this should be PARAPTOMA which is *"faults"* or *"trespasses."* There is a decided difference regarding confession.

Yes, 1 Peter 2:20 is HARMARTIA translated *"faults."* I think the best explanation is that though HARMARTIA can be *"faults"* or *"sins."* PARAPTOMA should be *"faults"* or *"trespasses,"* but not *"sins,"* especially when *"confession"* is involved.

"Easter" Or "Passover"?
QUESTION #202
Also, I was shocked that in Acts 12, it uses the word Easter instead of correct Passover, which casts a major doubt on the KJV supreme accuracy. Eventually, I concluded that the New King James Bible is quite an accurate translation and at the same time readable, corrects Acts 12 to use Passover, capitalizes pronouns referring to God and Jesus (He, Him, Us) and readable enough so I adopted it as my English Bible and have been reading it since.

ANSWER #202
I don't agree that the NKJV is superior to the KJB. You should get a *Defined King James Bible*. Uncommon words are defined accurately in the footnotes.

In Acts 12:3, *"then were the days of unleavened bread."* As a person with a Jewish background, you should be aware of the date of the feast of *"unleavened bread."* In Leviticus 23:6-7, we read:

23:6 "And on the **_fifteenth day_** of the same month is the feast of unleavened bread unto the LORD: seven days ye must eat unleavened bread."
7 "In the first day ye shall have an holy convocation: ye shall do no servile work therein."
You will also remember the date of the feast of passover. In Leviticus 23:5, we read:
Leviticus 23:5 we read:
"In the **_fourteenth day_** of the first month at even is the LORD'S passover."

Since the passover had already passed, the KJB translators referred to the pagan feast of Easter (which occurred at the same time as the Passover) rather than translating it "*passover*" as they have done in every other place where PASCHA occurs.

As you know, when you are in the 15th day of the month, it would be impossible for you to do something on the 14th day of the month which had already passed by.

If you still think the New KJV is superior to the accuracy of the KJB, you should get my documentary study of **BFT #1442 @ $10 + $7 S&H** where I show over 2,000 examples of the NKJV's adding to, subtracting from, or changing in other ways from the Hebrew, Aramaic, or Greek Words of the Bible.

The Authenticity Of Mark 16:9-20

QUESTION #203

I found something quite interesting in my KJV Study Bible. . What is your view of those twenty verses?

ANSWER #203

The MSS underlying some of the earliest versions or translations of the New Testament were based on older MSS than Vatican or Sinai because they preceded them both in date. The Vatican ("B") and Sinai (Aleph) manuscripts, according to Dean John W. Burgon, are the worst manuscripts that ever saw the light of day. For a complete and convincing defense of Mark 16:9-20, you should get *The Last Twelve Verses of Mark* (**BFT #1139 @ $16.00 + $7.00 S&H**). As far as false doctrines contained in Vatican and Sinai MSS, you should get Dr. Jack Moorman's book, *Early Manuscripts, Church Fathers, and the Authorized Version* (**BFT #3230 @ $20.00 + $7.00 S&H**). In this book, you will find almost 200 pages giving 356 doctrinal passages in the Vatican and Sinai MSS which are in doctrinal error. You should get this book as well.

N.T. "Judgment" And "Justice"
QUESTION #204
I'm having difficulty understanding the various notions of "*judgment*" in the KJB. Many modern translations have "*justice*" for "*judgment*" in several verses (i.e., Amos 5:7; Amos 5:24; etc.). When I think of anything concerning "*judgment*" I think of a courtroom in a negative way and when I think of anything concerning "*justice*" I think of a courtroom in a positive way. How can I tell what judgment actually means (positive or negative sense) in the KJB?

ANSWER #204
The word for judgment in the NT (KRISIS) is defined as below. It occurs 48 times in the AV and means various things, depending on the context.
2920 krisis {kree'-sis} perhaps a primitive word; TDNT - 3:941,469; n f
AV - judgment 41, damnation 3, accusation 2, condemnation 2; 48
1) a separating, sundering, separation
   1a) a trial, contest
2) selection
3) judgment
   3a) opinion or decision given concerning anything
      3a1) esp. concerning justice and injustice, right or wrong
   3b) sentence of condemnation, damnatory judgment, condemnation
      and punishment
4) the college of judges (a tribunal of seven men in the several
   cities of Palestine; as distinguished from the Sanhedrin,
   which had its seat at Jerusalem)
5) right, justice

The meaning in 1611 of "*judgment*" allows for all of the above meanings. In Amos 5:7 and 24, the meaning is obviously "*justice*" which in 1611 was included in "*judgment*."

Would Dean Burgon Revise The TR?
QUESTION #205
I have been reading Dean Burgon's "*The Revision Revised*" published by the Dean Burgon Society. The subtitle reads: "*A refutation of Westcott and Hort's false Greek Text and theory. A defense of the Authorised Version.*" Am I correct to say that Burgon seems to think that the Textus Receptus needs to be revised? What were his views on the TR? Did he hold the TR in high regard? Could you recommend to me a book giving Dean Burgon's views on the TR?

> **ANSWER #205**
>
> Dean Burgon thought there were some minor changes needed in the TR, but that, as it then stood, it would never lead any one seriously astray. My book, **BFT #804** (*Burgon's Warnings on Revision* @ $7.00 + $4.00 S&H) gives Burgon's quotes about revision of the Textus Receptus or the King James Bible. Unless the minor revision is done as Burgon specified, I believe that the Greek Words underlying the King James Bible should be left to stand as they are.

The Received Versus Critical Text

QUESTION #206

How many new words, verses, or passages have been found by the Critical Text camp since 1881 which differ from the English or Greek Text I would currently have (I have a TR and a Nestle 27). How much difference is there between the Westcott/Hort Text and the Nestle I have?

ANSWER #206

I don't know how many Nestle/Aland or UBS words are different from Westcott and Hort's Text, but they are very similar due to both group's following of the Vatican and Sinai MSS. An axiom of plain geometry applies here: "*Things equal to the same thing are equal to each other.*" I have a quote from Bruce Metzger himself who said that the NA and UBS committees "*began with the Westcott and Hort Greek Text*" and modified it as evidence dictated. I am sure there are a very small percentage of differences between the Westcott and Hort 1881 Greek text or that of either the Nestle-Aland or United Bible Societies Texts.

One important book on the differences between the TR and the CT is by Dr. Jack Moorman called *8,000 Differences Between the Critical Text and the Textus Receptus* (BFT #3084 @ $20.00 + $8.00 S&H).

Authorship of John's Gospel

QUESTION #207

How should I deal with a man who questions the authorship of the Gospel of John with much anger and meanness?

ANSWER #207

I believe that the apostle John was the writer of his Gospel, as well as 1 John, 2 John, 3 John, and Revelation. There are good reasons for this, but I think the most important question is how should you deal with this angry man.

> My strong advice to you is to deal with this skeptic as the Lord Jesus

My strong advice to you is to deal with this skeptic as the Lord Jesus Christ dealt with the scribes and Pharisees in Matthew 15:1 "*Then came to Jesus scribes and Pharisees, which were of Jerusalem, saying, . . .*" I believe the response of our Lord should be your response likewise. He told his disciples who were worried about the scribes and Pharisees being "*offended*" at His teaching: Matthew 15:12-14 tells how the Lord Jesus Christ dealt with such skeptics.

"*Then came his disciples, and said unto him, Knowest thou that the Pharisees were offended, after they heard this saying? 13 But he answered and said, Every plant, which my heavenly Father hath not planted, shall be rooted up. 14 **Let them alone**: they be blind leaders of the blind. And if the blind lead the blind, both shall fall into the ditch.*"

I believe we who are born-again Christians must apply over and over again, depending on the circumstances, those three little words of our Saviour: "*LET THEM ALONE.*" These words should ring in our ears and on our tongues whenever such a bothersome person comes with his or her skeptical questions. Especially if he has no idea whatever of conforming to truth, but only wants to bicker and battle. It doesn't matter whether the scorner is saved or lost, our response must be the same.

Another true and old saying also comes to mind: "*A man convinced against his will is of the same opinion still.*" You could use another saying, "*Let's agree to disagree without being disagreeable.*" But I don't think he wants to play that game. He loves to argue and be bitter. He sounds like an angry man. The Proverbs tells us in 22:24 "*Make no friendship with an angry man; and with a furious man thou shalt not go:*" This is good advice.

Once you settle this man on John, what about the many other books with no specified author? Where will it end? When will his contention stop? Proverbs 22:10 states: "*Cast out the scorner, and contention shall go out; yea, strife and reproach shall cease.*" **Only** if this man earnestly wishes to seek the truth, should you take your valuable time to lead him into that truth. Otherwise, "*Let him alone.*" It appears that answering this man's attitude is far more important than answering his question about the Apostle John and his writings.

The Sevenfold Spirit of God
QUESTION #208
I've been reading the book of Revelation again today and reading some commentaries about the seven Spirits of God in Rev. 4:5. Some suggested these might be angels, others that it represents the seven gifts or operations of the Spirit. What have been your thoughts about this?

ANSWER #208
As for the Revelation 4:5 and the "*seven spirits of God*," the usual interpretation of this phrase is found in Isaiah 11:1-2:

"*And there shall come forth a rod out of the stem of Jesse, and a Branch shall grow out of his roots: 2 And the* [1] **spirit of the LORD** *shall rest upon him, the* [2] *spirit of* **wisdom** *and* [3] **understanding***, the* [4] *spirit of* **counsel** *and* [5] **might***, the* [6] *spirit of* **knowledge** *and* [7] *of* **the fear of the LORD**;"

This indicates God the Holy Spirit's fulness and perfection I prefer this understanding to that of "*angels*."

Why Are There Various Wordings?
QUESTION #209
(1) Why are there 2 different accounts of what Jesus Christ said to the devil in the Wilderness?

Matthew 4:4 "*But he answered and said, It is written, Man shall not live by bread alone, but by every word that proceedeth out of the mouth of God.*"

Luke 4:4 "*And Jesus answered him, saying, It is written, That man shall not live by bread alone, but by every word of God.*" Which one did Jesus actually and really say? How do we reconcile this with the idea of Bible preservation?

ANSWER #209
I would answer it this way: Matthew had the full quotation, and Luke just summarized it for the Lord's own purpose as the Holy Spirit led him to write: "*every word . . . of God*" vs. "*every word that proceedeth out of the mouth of God*" The same Holy Spirit Who gave Matthew the Words gave Luke the Words and if He chose to vary those Words, there should be no problem. Just like He chose to vary the Words of the Old Testament many times when quoted in the New Testament.

The Meaning of "Written By"

QUESTION #210
At the end of some New Testament books, there is a phrase like "*written by*" and then a name. What does that "by" mean?

ANSWER #210
The DKJB includes the NT postscripts found in the 1611 KJV and in the Stephens Greek New Testament. For example, in the phrase "*written from Rome by Timothy*," the word "*by*" translates the Greek word DIA ("*through*"). DIA here (and elsewhere in the Romans through Hebrews postscripts) does not indicate the author but the carrier of the letter.

"Cephas," "Peter," And "Rock"

QUESTION #211
I have a few questions which I hope you can answer. I don't yet know Hebrew or Aramaic, and am not sure where to find my answers. Is there another word for "rock" in Aramaic, besides Cephas? What is the exact meaning of Cephas (Strong's just says, "the Rock"; is that it)? I saw in my Strong's that Cephas is related to the Hebrew "keph" (#3710), and that it is always a different Hebrew word used for "rock" when referring to God: does that mean anything? Also, would it be improper in the Greek to give a man a feminine name (i.e., to call Simon "*Petra*," rather than "*Petros*," if the Lord had so intended)? I would greatly appreciate your honest, careful answers to these questions.

ANSWER #211
I do not know if there is another Aramaic word for "*rock*" in addition to Cephas. There probably is, but I do not have an English/Aramaic dictionary. One Hebrew word for Rock is TSUWR which you probably already know. It is used of the Lord in Deuteronomy 32:4, and many other places. CELA is another. MAOWZ is another.

CEPHAS is masculine and PETROS is masculine (a name for Peter), but PETRA is feminine and is referring to the Lord Jesus Christ, not to Peter in Matthew 16:18. Objects in nature, like "*rock*," are either masculine, feminine, or neuter in various languages for unexplained reasons. They do not take on the human gender meanings, however.

Why The "Spirit Itself"?
QUESTION #212
Why do the King James Translators call the Holy Spirit an "*it*"?

ANSWER #212
Only in Romans 8:16 and 8:26 is the Holy Spirit referred to as "*itself*" in the King James Bible In all other places the KJB refers to the Holy Spirit with the pronoun, "*He*." The reason for the "*itself*" in these two verses is that the word for Spirit is PNEUMA which is a neuter noun in Greek. Grammatically the "*itself*" is accurate. John 16:8 and 16:13 are just two clear examples of the personality of God the Holy Spirit in the King James Bible.

Paul's Vow & Shaving His Head
QUESTION #213
In the Bible, there is an instance of where it talks of what Paul did to proclaim the gospel to the Jews. Paul became as the Jew and shaved his head (Acts 18:18) to visit the temple and proclaim the message. Was this right?

ANSWER #213
I don't think Paul was right in doing this. Somehow I believe the Lord must have rebuked him for it. It was the same general thing for which he scolded Peter (Galatians 2:11-12) for his hypocrisy in first eating with Gentiles and then not eating when the Jews came. I think tattooing is horrible for Christians to do regardless of their motives. I think the same of CCM, and/or "Christian" Rock in order to draw young people in. The same is true of the methods of Rick Warren's accommodations by putting theater seats in the auditorium and keeping silent about the gospel and many other doctrines.

A Defense of 1 John 5:7-8
QUESTION #214
Should 1 John 5:7-8 be in our New Testament as it appears in our King James Bible? Should I defend these verses from a man who wants to fight?

ANSWER #214
If I were you, I would either not answer him at all, or simply say that we must agree to disagree with him on this Greek grammatical point. He will not be persuaded no matter how many words you, or Dr. Moorman, or I might write him. I wonder how he gets around two external proofs: (1) those early church fathers and writers quoted from these verses. Where did they get them if they were not there when they lived? (2) hundreds of Latin manuscripts contain these verses in their entirety. How could this happen if they were not in

evidence from the very beginning? Remember this old saying, "*A man convinced against his will is of the same opinion still.*" Remember also the words of our Saviour who said of the Pharisees who were offended in his sayings.

Matthew 15: 13-14 "*But he answered and said, Every plant, which my heavenly Father hath not planted, shall be rooted up. 14 Let them alone: they be blind leaders of the blind. And if the blind lead the blind, both shall fall into the ditch.*"

These three words, "*Let them alone,*" scream out at me on various occasions, and I think this is one of them. It reminds me of Proverbs 29:9 in some ways: "*If a wise man contendeth with a foolish man, whether he rage or laugh, there is no rest.*" We might not be "*wise*" and he might not be a "*fool*," but I guarantee if you begin the long engagement with him in words, "*there will be no rest.*" I don't think either one of us has the time to win the unwinnable when there are so many other pressing duties facing us. The very first indication of this man's disingenuousness is the fact that he gave you no introduction as to his background, who he was, what he did for a living, whether he was saved or lost, a professor or a pastor and which church or school, whether in the GARBC, or some other group. The simple answer (which he will not accept) is "*We'll just have to agree to disagree on these matters. Thank you for your comments.*" He will want to continue the argument, but I would not respond further. Let him be infuriated if he wishes. The decision is yours.

> Dr. Moorman makes a good point on internal evidence from his article, p. 207 where he says:
>
>> "*The omission of the Johannine comma involves a grammatical difficulty. The words spirit, water, and blood are neuter in gender, but in 1 John 5:8 the spirit, the water, and the blood are personalized and that is the reason for the adoption of the masculine gender. But it is hard to see how such personalization would involve the change from the neuter to the masculine. For in verse 6 the word Spirit plainly refers to the Holy Spirit, the Third Person of the Trinity. Surely in this verse the word Spirit is 'personalized,' and yet the neuter gender is used. Therefore, since personalization did not bring about a change of gender in verse 6, it cannot fairly be pleaded as the reason for such a change in verse 8. If, however, the Johannine comma is retained, a masculine gender becomes readily apparent. It was due to the influence of the nouns Father and Word, which are masculine. Thus the hypothesis that the Johannine comma is an interpolation is full of difficulties.*"

"Indignation" and "Wrath"
QUESTION #215
In Romans 2:8, it says: *"But unto them that are contentious, and do not obey the truth, but obey unrighteousness, **indignation** and **wrath**,"* I don't really know the difference between indignation and wrath. Could you offer us suggestions with your Greek background?

ANSWER #215
The Greek word for "*indignation*" is THUMOS which means as follows:
2372 thumos {thoo-mos'}
from 2380; TDNT - 3:167,339; n m
AV - wrath 15, fierceness 2, indignation 1; 18
1) passion, angry, heat, **anger forthwith boiling up and soon subsiding again**
2) glow, ardour, the wine of passion, inflaming wine (which either drives the drinker mad or kills him with its strength)

The word for "*wrath*" is ORGE which means the following:
3709 orge {or-gay'}
from 3713; TDNT - 5:382,716; n f
AV - wrath 31, anger 3, vengeance 1, indignation 1; 36
1) anger, the natural disposition, temper, character
2) movement or agitation of the soul, impulse, desire, **any violent emotion, but esp. anger**
3) anger, wrath, indignation
4) anger exhibited in punishment, hence used for punishment itself
   4a) of punishments inflicted by magistrates

I prefer the **underlined** words for each Greek term if you have such in Chinese.

Modern Bibles' Failings
QUESTION #216
In Dr. Jack Moorman's *Missing in Modern Bibles: Is the Full Story Told?"* he says that codex B (the Vatican Manuscript) was written in Classical Greek. Is this true?

ANSWER #216
I have been told that "B" (the Gnostic Vatican Manuscript) is in classical Greek from various sources and though I have not checked it out, I would believe it. Dr. Moorman has studied this out and is, no doubt, correct. I do not know why it was written in classical Greek (if so) except that it came from Alexandria, Egypt which was one of the repositories of Classical Greek literature and learning.

I do know, however, that "B" and "Aleph" (Vatican and Sinai) are loaded down with over 356 doctrinal and historical errors due to the Gnostic Alexandrian heretics of the first 100 years after the N.T. was written. We must reject them as our final authority.

According to Dr. Moorman's study on *8000 Differences* (**BFT #3084** @ $20.00 + $8.00 S&H), there are over 8,000 differences between the Greek New Testament Vatican and Sinai manuscripts compared to those underlying the King James Bible.

The Meaning of PROS AUTON
QUESTION #217

Can you possibly help me with the following? It relates to an urgent dilemma regarding our translation into Romanian. What is the significance (if any!) of the usage of "PROS AUTON" following the verb "to say" ("LALEO" usually) as distinct from the simple dative (PROS AUTO with iota subscript) following "to say"? I checked Dana and Mantey as well as Robertson and didn't really find any particular help there.

ANSWER #217

I don't find any significant difference between PROS with the accusative AUTON and the dative of indirect object AUTO (with iota subscript). The KJB translation of PROS AUTON is always (in the several cases I checked) "*to him*" or "*to Him*" as the case may be. Would there be a significant difference in the Romanian language? I noted from Dana and Mantey that the root meaning of PROS is "*near or facing*." Perhaps the person speaking was "*near or facing*" the person addressed

Why "*Jeremy*" Not "*Jeremiah*"
QUESTION #218

I would like to know if you have any comment on Matthew 2:17. In various King James Bibles they have "*Jeremy.*" In others, they have "*Jeremiah.*" Why is this? Which is correct?

ANSWER #218

You cannot trust most KJB publishers for accuracy in names or other things. "*Jeremy*" is the correct transliteration of the Greek New Testament. "*Jeremiah*" is the correct transliteration in the Hebrew Old Testament, but not in the New Testament. Just about all of the Bible publishers and versions change words and spellings at will. The only two publishers you can trust for names are Oxford and Cambridge. However, Cambridge is better even than Oxford in all areas. This is why our DEFINED KING JAMES BIBLE uses the

Cambridge printed edition. It is (http://www.biblefortoday.org/kj_bibles.asp) They are under contract not to change anything, even spellings of words.

Males Praying In Mixed Meetings
QUESTION #219

In 1 Timothy 2:8, it says: "*I will therefore that **men** pray every where, lifting up holy hands, without wrath and doubting.*" What is the meaning of "*men*" here?

ANSWER #219

The root word for "*men*" is ANER. This is the masculine, nominative singular used as the subject of a sentence. Since ANER is the object of the verb, BOULOMAI ("*will, want, or desire*"), it is spelled ANDRAS. I believe that the only meaning of ANER is that of a male. It does not include females or others (as the Contemporary English Version renders it). The verse is therefore teaching that, in mixed audiences in the church or in other gatherings, that only males should lead in prayer. This verse would not prohibit women praying in women's gatherings.

Christ Abolished Moses' Law
QUESTION #220

In Matthew 5:17, the King James Bible has, "*Think not that I am come to DESTROY the law, or the prophets: I am not come to DESTROY, but to fulfill.*"

In Ephesians 2:15, the King James Bible has, "*Having ABOLISHED in his flesh the enmity, even the law of commandments contained in ordinances; for to make in himself of twain one new man, so making peace;*"

It has been charged that the there is a contradiction between Matthew 5:17 and Ephesians 2:15. Is there a way to harmonize these so that there is no contradiction?

ANSWER #220

The Lord Jesus Christ did fulfil the law of Moses, and, in effect, abolished that law for Christians today. We are not under any part of it because He abolished it for us.

The Meaning of Acts 2:38
QUESTION #221

I understand that "*shall receive*" in the Greek (& English) is future tense. Acts 2:38 says: "*Then Peter said unto them, Repent, and be baptized every one of you in the name of Jesus Christ for the remission of sins, and ye shall receive the gift of the Holy Ghost.*" The import of which is that the reception of the

Spirit is subsequent to baptism. What I am curious to know is: Had Luke, wanted to convey the idea of the simultaneous reception of the Spirit (i.e. at the point of baptism), can he convey that thought in Greek? If yes, how can this be done? If not, why not?

> ### ANSWER #221
>
> The future does indicate reception of the Holy Spirit after repentance and believer's baptism. The Greek language could express it clearer by using the present tense, *"you are receiving the gift of the Holy Ghost."* It is clear the way the Lord has written it, however.
>
> You must remember that Acts is a transitional book, and after the canon was completed, the Holy Spirit is now received the minute a person is born again and regenerated.

Another question that often comes up is the meaning of *"for"* in the phrase *"be baptized... for the remission of sins."* Those in the Church of Christ falsely teach that water baptism gives you *"the remission of sins."* This *"for"* as EIS in the Greek language can be taken in meanings #14 and #20 in the following list, that is, *"be baptized... because you have remission of sins."*

for [from *Webster's New World Dictionary*]
preposition
1 in place of; instead of [to use blankets for coats]
2 as the representative of; in the interest of [to act for another]
3 in defense of; in favor of [to fight for a cause, to vote for a levy]
4 in honor of [to give a banquet for someone]
5 with the aim or purpose of [to carry a gun for protection]
6 with the purpose of going to [to leave for home]
7 in order to be, become, get, have, keep, etc. [to walk for exercise, to fight for one's life]
8 in search of [to look for a lost article]
9 meant to be received by a specified person or thing, or to be used in a specified way [flowers for a girl, money for paying bills]
10 suitable to; appropriate to [a room for sleeping]
11 with regard to; as regards; concerning [a need for improvement, an ear for music]
12 as being [to know for a fact]
13 considering the nature of; as concerns [cool for July, clever for a child]
14 because of; as a result of [to cry for pain]
15 in proportion to; corresponding to [two dollars spent for every dollar earned]
16 to the amount of; equal to [a bill for $50]: when preceded and followed by the same noun, for indicates equality between things compared or contrasted (Ex.: dollar for dollar)

17 at the price or payment of [sold for $20,000]
18 to the length, duration, or extent of; throughout; through [to walk for an hour]
19 at (a specified time) [a date for two o'clock]
20 [Obs.] before conjunction--because; seeing that; since: more formal than because and used to introduce evidence or explanation for an immediately preceding statement [comfort him, for he is sad]

Questions On Matthew 24:36

QUESTION #222

I understand that Dean Burgon might have had something to say on the Greek wording of Matthew 24:36. In the KJV's English, the word "*but*" appears twice, but from vastly differing Greek: "DE" in the first case, and "EI ME" in the latter.

Something at the back of my mind suggests that it might have been Burgon who pointed out that EI ME is better translated "*unless*" (as Jerome had it in Latin in the Vulgate) and that gives off the opposite meaning to the traditional "*but the Father.*" Can you possibly help to clarify this?

ANSWER #222

I am sorry, but I do not know Dean Burgon's views on this verse. I prefer to leave it alone just as the traditional Greek Text has given it to us, despite what he might have written on it. You might search Dean Burgon's books on this if you have them in digital format. That's the only way to find this.

Hebrews 6:4-8 Explained

QUESTION #223

What is your interpretation of Hebrews 6:4-8? Please explain this passage.

ANSWER #223

I believe these are saved people who have received much light and then fall into sin and live for their flesh. They finally reach a state where it is impossible for them to "*repent*" and get back into fellowship with the Lord and live the rest of their lives "*saved yet so as by fire*" as it says in 1 Corinthians 3 at the Judgment seat of Christ. The "*better things*" are addressed to the saved people whom Paul hopes will not fall into sin and live for self, the world, and the devil, but instead will live for the Lord 100%.

The Work of God Holy Spirit

QUESTION #224

Romans 8:26 says:

> "*Likewise the Spirit also helpeth our infirmities: for we know not what we should pray for as we ought: but the Spirit itself maketh intercession for us with **groanings** which cannot be uttered.*"

Whose groanings are these groanings? Ours or Holy Spirit's? Or who groans, we or the Holy Spirit? Let me know. What does the Greek say?

ANSWER #224

The Greek text does not seem to give any positive clues. The clear sense of both the English and the Greek is that it is the Holy Spirit Who makes intercession with "*groanings.*" The "*for us*" (HYPER HUMON) is merely parenthetical and could be removed completely for the sense of it. God the Holy Spirit makes intercession with "*groanings*" that can't be uttered. The following verse, Romans 8:27, explains this further.

> "*And he that searcheth the hearts knoweth what is the mind of the Spirit, because he maketh intercession for the saints according to the will of God.*"

"*He Who searcheth the hearts*" is God the Father. He "*knoweth the mind of the Spirit*" Who is the One Who "*maketh intercession for us with **groanings** which cannot be uttered.*" But God the Father understands these groanings of the Spirit.

"Corporate Election" Explained

QUESTION #225

In the verse below (1 Peter 1:2) is the "*obedience*" our obedience or Jesus' obedience?

1 Peter 1:2 "*Elect according to the foreknowledge of God the Father, through sanctification of the Spirit, unto **obedience** and sprinkling of the blood of Jesus Christ: Grace unto you, and peace, be multiplied.*"

ANSWER #225

I believe it refers to the "*obedience*" of saved Christians, rather than the "*obedience*" of the Lord Jesus Christ. We're saved "*unto obedience.*" Salvation should result in "*obedience.*" I believe that when we are born-again by genuine faith in the Lord Jesus Christ, we become members of the Church which is Christ's chosen Body.

This Church, as a corporate Body, was chosen from "*before the foundation of the world*" (Ephesians 1:4). This is in accord with the foreknowledge of God the father and is through the sanctification of the Spirit unto (or resulting in) our "*obedience.*" Once we are saved, we come unto the efficacy of the "*sprinkling of the blood of Jesus Christ.*"

Hebrews 6:4 Refers To Christians

QUESTION #226

Hebrews 6:4 "*For it is impossible for those who were once enlightened, and have tasted of the heavenly gift, and were made partakers of the Holy Ghost, 5 And have tasted the good word of God, and the powers of the world to come, 6 If they shall fall away, to renew them again unto repentance; seeing they crucify to themselves the Son of God afresh, and put him to an open shame.*"

Who does "*if they shall fall away*" refer to? If we are truly saved, can we fall away? I know we fight with the flesh every day, every minute, every second. Can we go into our lust for a time?

ANSWER #226

I believe Paul is addressing Christian believers in Hebrews. In both Chapter 6 and 10, there are some seemingly difficult things to understand. I believe these Christians have drunk deeply into God's Words and are advanced in the faith. It speaks of "*drinking in the rain that cometh oft upon it.*" If this ground brings forth thorns instead of good fruit, these thorny works will be burned up as worthless.

I believe that "*fall away*" is to leave what they have been taught and depart from it. If this happens, they reach a point of carnality and worldliness whereby "*It is impossible*" (v. 4) "*to renew them again unto repentance.*" They do not lose their salvation, but perhaps the Lord in judging them might take them Home to heaven because He is so disappointed in their lives and because they are a very poor testimony to Him. This would be the "*sin unto death*" spoken of in 1 John 5:16.

Many have held that this passage refers to unsaved people, but the words used certainly imply that they are Christian believers who are advanced in the faith and then turn from those precious things they once held to and determine then to live for the world, the flesh and the devil instead of the Lord. This is a severe warning to saved people to keep on living for the Lord and not for self. Paul wanted to continue living for Christ lest he become a "*castaway*" or be "*laid on the shelf*" and not be used of the Lord any more. (1 Corinthians 9:27).

"Spirit" Or "spirit"?
QUESTION #227
1 John 5:8 *"And there are three that bear witness in earth, the Spirit, and the water, and the blood: and these three agree in one."*
Should this be "Spirit" or "spirit"?
ANSWER #227
As for the capitalization of the Holy Spirit, the Greek and Hebrew have no indication of what should be capitals. All the words are lower case. The capitals are all interpretation based on the context. I would capitalize "*Spirit*" in 1 John 5:8 because I think the reference is to God the Holy Spirit.

The Meaning Of "Might"
QUESTION #228
What does the word "*might*" mean in Romans 5:21,
"*That as sin hath reigned unto death, even so <u>might</u> grace reign through righteousness unto eternal life by Jesus Christ our Lord.*"
ANSWER #228
The "*might*" indicates that it is not a sure thing that all people would get eternal life, but only those who receive the Lord Jesus Christ as their Saviour in genuine faith will receive eternal life.

Meaning Of "Grace For Grace"
QUESTION #229
John 1:16 says: "*And of his fulness have all we received, and **grace for grace**.*"
The NASV, RSV, and the NRSV have "*grace upon grace.*" Does this "*for*" mean "*grace replacing grace*"?
ANSWER #229
The Greek word used representing "*for*" is "ANTI" which can mean, various things as listed below.
In Dana and Mantey's *Intermediate Grammar*, he indicates that often ANTI was used in the sense of "*in exchange for.*" This would be in line with "*instead of, or in place of.*" The sense of "*in exchange for*" would mean that of Christ's "*fulness have all we received*" and "*grace in exchange for grace*" in the sense of the following: Once we have exhausted Christ's grace, he gives us more grace in exchange for the previous grace and so on. There is a fulness of this grace which is inexhaustible and infinite. After the 2nd grace is exhausted, He exchanges it for more grace, and then more grace. It is like hot chocolate at some restaurants. When you empty one cup, they give you another cup in

exchange for the first one without charge. Then if you wish, they give you a 3rd cup in exchange for the 2nd cup, and so

473 anti {an-tee'}
a primary particle; TDNT - 1:372,61; prep
AV - for 15, because + 3639 4, for ... cause 1, therefore + 3639 1, in the room of 1; 22
1) over against, opposite to, before
2) for, instead of, in place of (something)
   2a) instead of
   2b) for
   2c) for that, because
   2d) wherefore, for this cause

Romans 1 And God's Words

QUESTION #230

Here is the question. In the first chapter of Romans, I see (hopefully correctly) an emphasis on God's Words. Paul references the Scriptures some 18-20 times at least in the 32 verses; for examples, other than the obvious references, here are some examples that I believe are there: His promises; the faith (which we cannot have without His Words); Christ is *"the power of God"* (1Cor. 1:23-24) who is the Word of God and whose words are powerful; revealed (reference to revelation in His words); *"things"* is often a translation of Hebrew, dabar, in the OT and is a reference to His words frequently in the NT; "judgment of God" is certainly based on His written Word (Jn 12:47-48); *"glory of God"* is a reference to His words in many places in Scripture and is linked by parallelism to verse 25 in Rom 1 (see the slide below). Anyway, I do not believe I have pushed the "envelope" of His Words beyond measure, but believe it is a secondary theme in chapter one, followed by the doctrinal explanations and applications of His Words in the rest of Romans.

ANSWER #230

Certainly in Romans 1, the Words of God underlie many of the problems found in that Chapter. The "*gospel*" must be founded on the Words, "*ungodliness*," and "*unrighteousness*" must be judged by the Words, the "*truth*" that they "*hold down*" is found in the Words, the "*glory of God*" is found in the Words, and the "*truth of God*" is found in the Words. Yes, underneath all of these things are the Words of God that have been rejected and denied.

Meaning of "Well Pleased"

QUESTION #231

Could you please tell me if "*well pleased*" in the KJV translated into "*pleased*" is accurate? I don't know in the KJV times if their "*well pleased*" is today's "*please*".

ANSWER #231

The word translated in the King James Bible as "*well pleased*" is in Greek as follows:
eudokeo {yoo-dok-eh'-o}
from 2095 and 1380; TDNT - 2:738,273; v
AV - be well pleased 7, please 5, have pleasure 4, be willing 2,
    be (one's) good pleasure 1, take pleasure 1, think good 1; 21
1) it seems good to one, is one's good pleasure
  1a) think it good, choose, determine, decide
  1b) to do willingly
  1c) to be ready to, to prefer, choose rather
2) to be well pleased with, take pleasure in, to be favourably
    inclined towards one

Notice, it comes from #2095 ("well":) and #1380 "dokeo" which is as follows:
1380 dokeo {dok-eh'-o}
a prolonged form of a primary verb, doko {dok'-o} (used only in
    an alternate in certain tenses; cf the base of 1166) of
    the same meaning; TDNT - 2:232,178; v
AV - think 33, seem 13, suppose 7, seem good 3, please 2, misc 5; 63
1) to be of opinion, think, suppose
2) to seem, to be accounted, reputed
3) it seems to me
  3a) I think, judge: thus in question
  3b) it seems good to, pleased me, I determined

For Synonyms see entry 5837

    The word "*pleased*" leaves off the "*well*" which is a part of the Greek word EUDOKEO. The EU is the "*well*" and should be translated as such. Are you just "*pleased*" with your wife or are you "*well pleased*"?

James 5:16 And Bruce Metzger

QUESTION #232

1. The pastor of my church held a forum on Bible versions. They don't preach from the King James. I disagree with them. A member asked a question on James 5:16. He asked them why the word translated *"faults"* in the KJB is not *"sins"* as in modern versions. Could you explain why *"faults"* is the better word?

2. He asked about the textual scholar Metzger and his belief that the Old Testament is filled with errors and myths. One pastor that attended Princeton said that he had met and talked with Metzger and said this is true. After talking to him he thought that Metzger was right on the atonement and who Jesus is. I think my pastor is wrong.

ANSWER #232

In James 5:16, the Gnostic Critical Greek Text reads "*sins*" which is wrong. The Textus Receptus correctly reads "*faults*." If the verse reads "*sins*," this makes provision for the Roman Catholic Confessional which is unscriptural. Bruce Metzger is wrong on the Bible's having errors and myths. He is also wrong on who Jesus is and on the atonement. He was a modernist liberal infidel. His Bible was a seriously flawed Bible. Because of this he also has a flawed Christology.

1 Timothy 5:14 And "Women"

QUESTION #233

A friend told us her pastor told her that 1 Timothy 5:14, in the original Greek, doesn't have the word "*women*." I don't know how to answer her. Please help me.

*"I will therefore that the **younger women** marry, bear children, guide the house, give none occasion to the adversary to speak reproachfully."*

ANSWER #233

While it is true that "*women*" does not occur, the word used is NEOTERAS. This is a feminine plural form. It is therefore very properly translated *"younger women."* If it were a masculine plural, it would be properly translated *"younger men."*

What TR Before Beza's 5th in 1598?
QUESTION #234
In your book, *Defending the King James Bible*, you said that the 5th edition of Beza's Text came out in 1598 and this was the Greek edition used as the basis of the King James Bible. What did they use before that?

ANSWER #234
The first printed form of the Received Text was that of Erasmus in 1516. He had many other editions. Martin Luther used one of Erasmus' editions for his German translation. The Complutensian Polyglot was edited by Cardinal Ximenes and was published in Acala, Spain. It was called a "polyglot" because it contained a number of languages in addition to the Greek. That was completed in 1514, but wasn't circulated until 1522. Actually the first Greek New Testament to be completed was the Complutensian Polyglot. Erasmus' edition was completed a little later, but was printed earlier, that is, in 1516. Once the printing press got into use, the changes were not as great, because the editions would be type-set. Before that, they just had to use handwritten manuscripts. These manuscripts were handwritten, not in printed form, being copies of copies, beginning with the original Greek New Testament writings.

"Study" In 2 Timothy 2:15
QUESTION #235
In 2 Timothy 2:15, what does the word "*study*" mean?

ANSWER #235
I think "*diligence*" is involved in "*study*" as even the 1828 Webster Dictionary mentions ("*3. To endeavor diligently.*") Below, you can see that SPOUDAZO occurs 11 times in the KJB NT and you'll notice even 5 times it is either "'*do diligence*," "*be diligent*" or "*give diligence*."

4704 spoudazo {spoo-dad'-zo}
from 4710; TDNT - 7:559,1069; v
AV - endeavour 3, do diligence 2, be diligent 2, give diligence 1,
  be forward 1, labour 1, study 1; 11
1) to hasten, make haste
2) to exert one's self, endeavour, give diligence

"Book Of Life" vs. "Tree Of Life"

QUESTION #236

Could you please tell me how to respond to someone who says that Revelation.22:19 should say "*tree of life*" instead of "*book of life*"? Most commentaries also say that "*tree of life*" is in most Greek manuscripts.

ANSWER #236

There is good evidence for "*book of life*" as found in Dr. Jack Moorman's book, *When the KJV Departs From the 'Majority Text'*, pp. 113-14 (**BFT #1617** @ $16.00 + $6.00 S&H). Reference is also made by him on p. 312 of his book, *Early Manuscripts, Church Fathers, and the Authorized Version* (**BFT #3230** @ $20.00 + $6.00 S&H) The "*tree*" of life would make no sense, as Dr. Moorman mentions. You will never convince those on the critical Text side that their text is wrong. It appears to be a waste of time. You can have every confidence in the Greek and Hebrew Words underlying the KJB.

The Errors Of Dan Wallace

QUESTION #237

I was watching a video on the DaVinci code from the Radio Bible Class as hosted by Mark DeHaan. There was a segment on manuscripts with Dr. Daniel Wallace. He stated that we have earlier manuscripts from the fourth century that make the King James Bible manuscripts outdated. Also have you heard of Dr. Daniel Wallace?

ANSWER #237

Dan Wallace is dead wrong that early 4th century manuscripts make the KJB Bible outdated. I know of him by his many articles that mercilessly attack the KJB and its underlying Hebrew, Aramaic, and Greek Words. He is a graduate of Dallas Theological Seminary as I also am and now teaches at that Seminary. You can read at http://www.deanburgonsociety.org/News/no_75.htm the answer of Dr. Jack Moorman to some of Wallace's errors on the Bible.

Mark 3:28 And John 1:42

QUESTION #238

Can you help me in my translation:
1) I have difficulty in Mark 3:28:
    a) I don't know how to distinguish: BLASPHEMIA (G988) from BLASPHEMEO? (G987).
    b) Does the "SONS OF MEN" just mean "ALL MEN"?
2) CEPHAS (G2786) and PETROS (G4074) in John 1:42: "*which is by*

Questions on the New Testament and Its Texts

interpretation, A stone." What kind of stone/rock are they?

ANSWER #238

1. a. BLASPHEMIA is a noun and BLASPHEMEO is a verb that carries out the meaning of the noun which means: 1) slander, detraction, speech injurious, to another's good name; 2) impious and reproachful speech injurious to divine majesty.

b. Yes, the term, "*sons of men*," means human beings in general.

2. CEPHAS is an Aramaic word meaning "*stone.*" We're not sure how large it was. PETROS means also "*a rock or a stone.*" PETRA (Matthew 16:18) is a large rock or stone, or a boulder.

"Should Not" In John 12:40

QUESTION #239

I am working in Gospel of John. I do not understand John 12:40: "*He hath blinded their eyes, and hardened their heart; that they should not see with their eyes, nor understand with their heart, and be converted, and I should heal them.*"

Can I understand in the following way: Their sins have caused God to let them alone and not be converted? Can HINA ME, which is translated "*should not*," be understood as "*lest*"?

ANSWER #239

Your explanation is a good one. In God's foreknowledge He knew that these people would not accept Him and did not want to accept Him. Their state was one of "*blindness*" but God still holds them responsible for rejecting His Son and His salvation. He would like for them to be saved, but they refused to "*see,*" therefore they were as blind people in their rejection of light. It is a difficult thing to comprehend. HINA ME could be understood as "*lest.*"

"Temptation" Versus "Trial"

QUESTION #240

Please help me to resolve the differences between "*temptation*" and "*trial.*"

ANSWER #240

Temptation is PEIRASMOS. It can mean various things, depending on the context. Here are some of the various meanings of this word:
1) an experiment, attempt, trial, proving
  1a) trial, proving: the trial made of you by my bodily condition, since condition served as to test the love of the Galatians toward Paul (Gal. 4:14)
  1b) the trial of man's fidelity, integrity, virtue, constancy
    1b1) an enticement to sin, temptation, whether arising from

the desires or from the outward circumstances
- 1b2) an internal temptation to sin
  - 1b2a) of the temptation by which the devil sought to divert Jesus the Messiah from his divine errand
- 1b3) of the condition of things, or a mental state, by which we are enticed to sin, or to a lapse from the faith and holiness
- 1b4) adversity, affliction, trouble: sent by God and serving to test or prove one's character, faith, holiness
- 1c) temptation (i.e. trial) of God by men
  - 1c1) rebellion against God, by which his power and justice are, as it were, put to the proof and challenged to show themselves

Quite often *"temptation"* (like the *"temptation"* of the Lord Jesus Christ) is merely a *"testing."* It does not imply any sinful connotation. So, sometimes the context indicates a positive mere *"testing,"* and in other contexts it means a *"sinful enticement to sin."*

The Date Of The "Textus Receptus"

QUESTION #241

I have been in a debate with an individual about the usefulness of the Textus Receptus. The date of its publication came into play. I was wondering if you could tell me exactly when and by whom this document was printed.

ANSWER #241

The Textus Receptus, as a name, was a Latin phrase first used by Bonaventure and Abraham Elzevir, in their 1633 edition. They said this about their edition of the Greek text: "**Textum** ergo habes, nunc ab omnibus **receptum**" -- "*So* [the reader] *has the text which all now received.*" The Elzevir brothers merely said that their Greek text was a text that had been through the previous many years *"ab omnibus receptum"* that is, *"by all received"* or *"received by all."* This has nothing whatsoever to do with the origin of what is called the *"Textus Receptus."* In point of fact, this has been the Greek text that had its origin from the original writings in the Apostolic Times themselves and had continuity from that time right up to the publication of the Elzevir Greek New Testament in 1633. The Received Text underlying the King James Bible is that of Beza's 5th edition of 1598 as used by Dr. Frederick Scrivener.

"Study Bible" Recommendation

QUESTION #242
I am looking to purchase a study Bible. Is there any that you recommend?

ANSWER #242
I recommend our *Defined King James Bible* though some would not call it a "*study Bible.*" Uncommon words are defined accurately in the footnotes. To that extent it is a "*study Bible.*" Other than that one, I don't believe there are any safe "*study Bibles*" that I am aware of. They all have problems.

I have always used the Old Scofield Reference Bible (Not the new one). There are a few notes with which I would disagree, but I disagree 100% with any changes they suggest you make in the words of the King James Bible. Scofield was smitten with the false Gnostic Critical Greek Text and changed many KJB words to conform to this erroneous text. Don't follow any of these changes. Otherwise their notes are very helpful.

"With" In Mark 10:27

QUESTION #243
Mark 10:27 says: "*And Jesus looking upon them saith,* **With** *men it is impossible, but not with God: for with God all things are possible.*" What is behind the meanings of the preposition "*with*"?

ANSWER #243
As far as "*with*" in Mark 10:27, the Greek word used is PARA. It has the following meanings:
3844 para {par-ah'}
a root word; TDNT - 5:727,771; prep
AV - of 51, with 42, from 24, by ... side 15, at 12, than 11,
    misc 45; 200
1) from, of at, by, besides, near
    The meaning of PARA here is "*as for God*" or "*as far as God is concerned*" or "*in the case of God.*" "*With*" is one of the proper meanings.

Why "Which" In 1 John 1:1?

QUESTION #244
I am teaching in John's First General Epistle. I have a question on I John 1:1 which says: "*That* **which** *was from the beginning,* **which** *we have heard,* **which** *we have seen with our eyes,* **which** *we have looked upon, and our hands have handled, of the Word of life;*" My question is, why didn't they translate it by a masculine article instead of the neuter article?

ANSWER #244

The *"which"* is used because the article, HO, is a neuter, not a masculine article. The same is true for 1 John 1:3. The neuter could refer in abstract (expressing a quality) to both animate and inanimate The first *"that which was from the beginning"* could refer to the fact that John was there in the beginning of the Lord's ministry. Or it could refer, as in verse 2, to *"the life"* (which is abstract and therefore demands a *"which"* not a *"who."*) Then it says, "we heard,.. we saw,.. we looked upon,.. our hands handled–of the Word of life." That *"Word of life"* is a title of the Lord which could be abstract (expressing a quality and grammatically a neuter idea, but interpretively a masculine reference to the Lord) and therefore thought of as a *"that which."*

Then "*the life*" was manifested (an abstract concept applied to the Lord, but still abstract--expressing a quality), and we saw it (this life, though a Person, still an abstract quality), and bear witness and show you that eternal life. This is an abstract Name for the Lord, thus it could **grammatically** be neuter, but **interpretively** be personal . You can speak of "*the life which*" and not necessarily would have to say "*the life who.*"

This is similar to the grammatical translation of "*it*" referring to the Holy Spirit yet He is a person. Translationally, He is a Person, but AUTO is Neuter and so grammatically the KJB rendered it "*it*" (Romans 8:16 and 8:26).

Which Greek Interlinear N.T.?

QUESTION #245

I have been looking at two Interlinear Greek-English New Testaments: (1.) By George Ricker Berry (with the Greek Stephanus Edition) and (2.) By Jay P. Green (with the Greek Scrivener Edition of Beza's 5th edition, 1598). Of the two books which one would be a better choice?

ANSWER #245

I prefer the one by George Ricker Berry because, although it uses the Stephens Greek, and though it is not perfect, it has the KJB in the margin. At least you can see the Greek Words and look them up elsewhere if needed. He uses Stephens 1550 Greek text which is not as good as the TBS/Scrivener used by Jay Green's Interlinear.

Jay Green uses the TR/Scrivener's Text which is the best, but he uses his own translation in the margins which is far inferior to the KJB.

Both of these are useful to find out the Hebrew and Greek Words underlying the King James Bible.

Acts 13:48 And Hyper-Calvinism
QUESTION #246
I have a question on Acts 13:48: *"And when the Gentiles heard this, they were glad, and glorified the word of the Lord: and as many as were ordained to eternal life believed."*

The word *"ordained"* has been attacked because it seems to smack too strongly of Reformed theology. These people teach that only those who are predestined to eternal life will believe. They use this verse to prove their theory. Do you have any comments that you could send along to help?

ANSWER #246
The Greek word in Acts 13:48 for "*ordained*" is TASSO. It means: *"(1) to put in order, to station; 1a) to place in a certain order, to arrange, to assign a place, to appoint; 1a1) to assign (appoint) a thing to one; 1b) to appoint, ordain, order; 1b1) to appoint on one's own responsibility or authority; 1b2) to appoint mutually, i.e. **agree upon**."*

If you take the meaning of "*as many as 'agreed upon' eternal life believed*," it would make sense. They agreed that eternal life was something they needed. They agreed that the conditions for eternal life were receiving the Lord Jesus Christ who died for their sins as Saviour. Because they agreed on these things that were preached to them, they believed on the Lord Jesus Christ and were saved. This would then be in line with the hundreds of verses that predicate eternal life and salvation upon genuine believing, rather than upon being predestinated or elected to it.

In fact, the order in the Greek text is "*they believed, (that is) as many as agreed upon eternal life.*" This shows that they believed about something that they agreed upon, that is, the conditions of receiving eternal life.

Mark 16:9-20–Right Or Wrong?
QUESTION #247
I am greatly appreciative of the many things you said on both Mk 16:9-20 and other subjects. I wish to consult you in an area which is your learned expertise. Recently I came across the following two objections to the Long Ending of Mk 16:

(1) There is no instance of the typical Marcan stylistic transitions or methods (such as beginning a phrase with a parataxis).

(2) Overall, the passage has the "*distinct flavour of the second century*" and appears to be a pastiche of material taken from other Gospels. [See for this data Markan commentaries by Brooks (272-3), Lane (601-4), and Anderson (358).]

What does objection (1) mean? Did you or anyone else deal with this objection? If not, kindly direct me to a source where the treatment of the objection is both thorough and easily understood. By the way, has this objection been dealt with in Burgon's book on *The Last Twelve Verses of Mark*?

As for objection (2), let me know your learned judgment on the comments by the various scholars listed. Is there any source dealing effectively with this objection?

ANSWER #247

Dean Burgon's *LAST 12 VERSES OF MARK* (**BFT #1139** @ $15.00 + $5.00 S&H) takes up both these objections.

(1) The style is definitely that of Mark. He shows this by a comparison of other places in Mark.

(2) The "*flavour*" is that of first century and had to have been written then to have had the following facts be true (as Dean Burgon shows):

(a) 18 Uncials have it (only "B" and "Aleph" (Vatican and Sinai) omit it in Burgon's day);

(b) about 600 cursives have it;

© every known Lectionary of the East has it.

(d) ten early translations have it (many of whom were made prior to Vatican and Sinai).

(e) nineteen early church fathers quoted from it (many of whom lived prior to Vatican and Sinai's dates. I strongly urge you to get that book. I would pay no heed whatever to Brooks, Lane, and Anderson who have not done their homework as Dean Burgon has. His book has never been answered.

Translation Of Verses In Mark
QUESTION #248

Here are some questions we cannot decide during our translation:

1) Mark 13:8 "*For nation shall rise against nation, and kingdom against kingdom.*" Can it be understood as: people of the world against people of God, and kingdom of the world against kingdom of God?

2) Mark 13:25 "*And the stars of heaven shall fall, and the powers that are in heaven shall be shaken.*" "*The powers that are in heaven.*" Can it be translated as "*power of the air,*" as in Ephesians 2:2.

3) Mark 15:2 "*And Pilate asked him, Art thou the King of the Jews? And he answering said unto him, Thou sayest it.*" Which way is right for "*Thou sayest it*"? a) "*This is what you say,*" or b) "*what you say is right.*"

ANSWER #248

(1) I don't see any reason to make it "*kingdom of God.*" Since "*nation*" precedes it, I believe it refers to "*kingdom*" in the sense of possibly more than one nation united into a "*kingdom.*" Like the alliances in Europe and the United Nations, etc. They would be "*kingdoms*" since there are more than one "*nation*" involved.

(2) I think that "*heaven*" should be used. Remember, there are at least 3 "*heavens*" in the Bible: (1) the 1st "*heaven*" is the atmospheric "*heaven*" above the earth; (2) the 2nd "*heaven*" is the starry heaven above our atmosphere, and (3) the 3rd "*heaven*" is God's Home (2 Corinthians 12:2). The Ephesians 2:2 "*air*" would confine it only to the "*atmospheric heaven*" where Satan operates. "*Heaven*" should be used and it would indicate both the 1st and 2nd "*heavens.*"

I believe it is "*what you say is right.*" When Jesus told Pilate "*Thou sayest it,*" He meant the answer was "*Yes.*" He agreed with Pilate that He was and is the King of the Jews.

Blasphemy Against the Holy Spirit
QUESTION #249

I was reading the Gospel of Matthew again this weekend and a question came back to me that I never was able to figure out.

Matthew 12:32 says: "*And whosoever speaketh a word against the Son of man, it shall be forgiven him: but whosoever speaketh against the Holy Ghost, it shall not be forgiven him, neither in this world, neither in the world to come.*"

When the Lord speaks of the blasphemy of the Holy Ghost. I don't wonder so much what that blasphemy is, but rather how is it all right to speak against the Lord Jesus Christ, but not against the Holy Ghost, since both are God?

ANSWER #249

I like to explain this as follows: I do not believe that blasphemy against the Holy Spirit can be committed today in the same way as then. (1) Then, it was attributing the works of the Lord Jesus Christ to Satan. (2) Now, it is rejecting the Holy Spirit's convicting power to receive the Lord Jesus Christ as Saviour.

Beza's 5th Edition (1598) Is Superior

QUESTION #250

How can you insist on only Beza 5th edition 1598 Text, and not other texts of the same family?

ANSWER #250

It is true that I believe Beza's 5th edition, 1598, was the edition used by the KJB in over 99% of the cases. This edition was 82 years after that of Erasmus in 1516. According to Dr. F. H. A. Scrivener, the KJB translators used this edition in all but about 190 passages. He has listed these passages in his APPENDIX. You can see Dr. Scrivener's book by ordering Scrivener's *Annotated Greek New Testament* (**BFT #1670 @ $35.00 + $5.00 S&H**). My position is that the Hebrew, Aramaic, and Greek Words underlying the KJB are the Words God has preserved for us and are the exact Words of the originals themselves.

Ephesians 2:8-9 Explained Clearly

QUESTION #251

Ephesians 2:8-9 says: *"For by grace are ye saved through __faith__; and __that__ not of yourselves: it is the __gift__ of God: Not of works, lest any man should boast."*

I had been told that my *"faith"* was a "*gift*" from God too. I bought into that theory. Before that, I believed the *"faith"* was mine! Which is correct, God's *"faith,"* or my *"faith."* Do you have something in layman's terms to explain this?

ANSWER #251

In the New Testament Greek grammar, pronouns must agree with their antecedent nouns in gender. Many Bible teachers, especially those who are hyper-Calvinists, teach that the word, *"faith,"* is the noun to which the pronoun, *"that,"* refers. This is grammatically impossible and therefore theologically incorrect to teach that.

The clear reason for this is as follows: The gender of the noun, *"faith,"* (HE PISTIS) is feminine. The gender of pronoun, that (TOUTO) is neuter. This pronoun, TOUTO, refers back to the entire concept of being *"saved"* (SESOSMENOI). When this true antecedent of TOUTO is seen to be the concept of being *"saved,"* the entire verse makes sense. The reference of *"that"* (TOUTO) is **not** to *"faith"* which is *"not of yourselves, it is the gift of God: not of works lest any man should boast."* The reference is, **rather**, being *"saved"* and *"salvation"* that is *"not of yourselves, it is the gift of God: not of works lest any man should boast."*

Holy "Ghost" Or Holy "Spirit"?
QUESTION #252
In the King James Bible, why is the Greek word, PNEUMA, sometimes referred to as the *"Holy Spirit"* and sometimes referred to as the *"Holy Ghost"*?
ANSWER #252
Both *"spirit"* and *"ghost"* words are correct and meant the same thing in 1611. There has been no definitive answer given so far as I know. Some say that *"Holy Ghost"* was used when special emphasis was made as His being the Third Person of the Trinity. "Ghost" is an ecclesiastical term of God the Holy Spirit used in 1611 in a very respectful manner. As you know, *"Holy Ghost"* is also used in the Doxology that is currently sung in many churches around the world today.

The Holy Spirit Before Pentecost
QUESTION #253
How was the Holy Ghost that Jesus gave to his disciples in John 20:22 different from that which they received on the day of Pentecost?

I've heard some teach that the church didn't actually exist until that day, yet the Lord speaks of it as if it already existed in Matthew 18:17.
ANSWER #253
John 20:20-22 says:
20 *And when he had so said, he shewed unto them his hands and his side. Then were the disciples glad, when they saw the Lord.*
21 *Then said Jesus to them again, Peace be unto you: as my Father hath sent me, even so send I you.*
22 *And when he had said this, he breathed on them, and saith unto them, Receive ye the Holy Ghost*:

The disciples were given the Holy Spirit to be with them on a temporary basis (as in the O.T.). On the day of Pentecost, the Holy Spirit was received on a permanent basis and so throughout this church age. In this, the Lord fulfilled His promise when he said, John 14:17 "*Even the Spirit of truth; whom the world cannot receive, because it seeth him not, neither knoweth him: but ye know him; for he dwelleth with you, and shall be in you.*"

As far as the beginning of the *"church,"* some are teaching falsely that the church began either with John the Baptist or when the Lord Jesus Christ was still on the earth. In Matthew 16:18, the "*church*" is clearly yet future. The

Lord Jesus Christ said very clearly in the future tense in the Greek text, "*I will build my church.*" He did not say, "*I have already built my church.*" He did not say "*John the Baptist already built my church.*" He said He would "*build*" it but at some time in the future. True, the root and basis was the Lord Jesus Christ Himself, but the full grown entity was on the Day of Pentecost when God the Holy Spirit came upon the Christians in power and indwelt them with His permanent presence.

> I realize that there are many of our Baptist brethren who erroneously teach (as I said before) that the church began with either John the Baptist or the Lord Jesus Christ, but while this might be true in seed form, the plant was made at Pentecost.

This is what I believe to be true for many reasons, yet I give the other brethren the right to differ on this. Christ became the Head of the church based upon His crucifixion, burial, bodily resurrection, and ascension. Until He ascended and the Holy Spirit descended as the "*other Comforter,*" the church was not fully formed.

Bible Preservation
QUESTION #254

Bible preservation is the idea that God has kept His Words intact from generation to generation. Can a Biblical writer choose to vary the words of the Holy Spirit? If so, is he not adding or subtracting from what God said?

ANSWER #254

"*Biblical writers*" never chose any of the Hebrew, Aramaic, or Greek Words that they wrote. Every Word was chosen by God the Holy Spirit Who, in turn, received those Words from the Lord Jesus Christ. If there seems to be a variation in wording anywhere in the Bible, it was not the "*Biblical writer*" who varied it, but God the Holy Spirit and God the Son who did so. And we must never question these variations that God, for His own reasons and purposes, has set forth in the Bible.

Old Testament Quotes In The N.T.
QUESTION #255

You mentioned in your first reply the fact that NT writers often included varied quotations from the Old Testament.

I am reading the Reese Chronological Bible so this problem is highlighted even more. Since you will read Matthew, Mark, and Luke all saying Jesus said something and when they quote Jesus they all quote him saying the same thing differently. Why is this?

Questions on the New Testament and Its Texts 35

ANSWER #255
The four Gospels, as some have stated, are like four blind men describing an elephant. They all are on different parts of that animal and describe it differently. The Lord Jesus Christ spoke on many occasions and I am sure He stated things in slightly different ways on each of those occasions. The Gospel writers were led of the Holy Spirit to state what He said on those occasions exactly as he spoke them, and I believe they did.

What Is A "Neighbour"?
QUESTION #256
There is a translation which is different from KJB: "*love thy neighbour as thyself*" is translated as "*love others as thyself*" in Leviticus 19:18, Matthew 19:19; 22:39, Mark 12:31, Romans 13:9, Galatians 5:14, and James 2:8. In Greek, can it be translated as "*others*" or "*man*" as well as "*neighbor*"? Because in Luke 10:36 Jesus explained to the lawyer that he was the neighbor, so "*love thy neighbour as thyself*" signifies great meanings.

ANSWER #256
In Matthew 19:19, and in these other verses, the word for "*neighbour*" is PLESION. Its various meanings are listed below:

4139 plesion {play-see'-on}
neuter of a derivative of pelas (near); TDNT - 6:311,872; adv
AV - neighbour 16, near 1; 17
1) a neighbour
  1a) a friend
  1b) any other person, and where two are concerned, the other
    (thy fellow man, thy neighbour), according to the Jews, any
    member of the Hebrew race and commonwealth
  1c) according to Christ, any other man irrespective of race or
    religion with whom we live or whom we chance to meet

> In every verse you quoted, PLESION is used and carries with it the preceding meanings. It would seem like the word "*neighbour*" or "*friend*" or "*thy fellow man*" or "*any other man with whom we live or whom we chance to meet*" would be the sense.

ANSWER #235

The blind "experts" assume have stated, are like four blind men describing an elephant. They all err on different parts of that animal and described differently. The Lord Jesus Christ spoke on many occasions, and I'm sure He spoke to men in all fifty different ways on each of those occasions. The Gospel writers were led of the Holy Spirit to show what He said and how He chose to say it on each subject he spoke.

CHAPTER II
QUESTIONS ON THE O.T.
& HEBREW SUBJECTS

O.T. Meaning Of "Judgment"

QUESTION #257
I noticed that you provided a Greek definition of "*judgment*". I'm curious about this--what would be the Hebrew understanding.

ANSWER #257
Here is the Hebrew term. It is less clear in the Hebrew, SHEPHET. Context must govern the flavor of that word:
08201 shephet {sheh'-fet}
from 08199; TWOT - 2443a; n m
AV - judgment 16; 16
1) judgment, act of judgment

Psalm 119's Hebrew Letters

QUESTION #258
We would like to know what the different marks in Psalm 119 mean. It is a mark, usually different for each section, and then different name as "coph, lamed," etc. We have tried to look this up in different references but have not found an answer. Please tell us what is meant by them.

ANSWER #258
The 176 verses of Psalm 119 are divided into 22 sections of 8 verses each (8 x 22 = 176). This is one 8-verse section for each of the 22 letters in the Hebrew language. At the beginning of each 8-verse section is one of the 22 letters of the Hebrew alphabet, beginning with ALEPH, then BETH, then GIMMEL and all the way down to TAU, the last letter in the Hebrew alphabet. In the Hebrew text, each verse in the 8-verse section begins with the Hebrew letter shown at the beginning of that section. For example, each of the eight

verses in Psalm 119:1-8 begins with the Hebrew letter ALEPH.

The Teachings of Psalm 23:5

QUESTION #259

What is Psalm 23:5 specifically teaching?

"*Thou preparest a table before me in the presence of mine enemies: thou anointest my head with oil; my cup runneth over.*"

ANSWER #259

I believe David was assured that God would provide him food (the "*table*") even among his enemies. His head was "*anointed*" because he was the king of Israel. All kings were anointed. His "*cup*" running over shows that his blessings were overflowing in great abundance. Pastor D. A. Waite.

Jeremiah's "Lost" Words & the KJB

QUESTION #260

I have some questions concerning favoritism. I was wondering if you could give me some Scripture about it? Also can you give me some Scripture about pastors gossiping to other pastors?

ANSWER #260

Here are a few verses against "*favoritism*" or having "*respect of persons.*"

Acts 10:34 "*Then Peter opened his mouth, and said, Of a truth I perceive that God is **no respecter of persons**:*"

2 Chronicles 19:17 "*And if ye call on the Father, who **without respect of persons** judgeth according to every man's work, pass the time of your sojourning here in fear*:"

Proverbs 24:23 "*These things also belong to the wise. It is **not good to have respect of persons** in judgment.*"

Proverbs 28:21 "***To have respect of persons is not good***: *for for a piece of bread that man will transgress.*"

Romans 2:11 "*For there is **no respect of persons with God**.*"

Ephesians 6:9 "*And, ye masters, do the same things unto them, forbearing threatening: knowing that your Master also is in heaven; **neither is there respect of persons with him**.*"

Colossians 3:25 "*But he that doeth wrong shall receive for the wrong which he hath done: and **there is no respect of persons**.*"

James 2:1 "*My brethren, **have not** the faith of our Lord Jesus Christ, the Lord of glory, **with respect of persons**.*"

1 Peter 1:17 "*And if ye call on the Father, who **without respect of persons** judgeth according to every man's work, pass the time of your sojourning here in fear:*"

Interpretation of Isaiah 55:11-13

QUESTION #261

When you have time, could you examine the Hebrew text in Isaiah 55:11-13. The question I have is does the "*it*" in 55:13 refer back to the four "*its*" in 55:11 and therefore "*my words*" in 55:11. If that is correct, I plan to write a paper on the sign, its purity, eternality, etc, like the attributes of the second person of the Trinity as a sign of the Lord Jesus Christ, left on earth to signify Him and His beauty.

ANSWER #261

The four "*its*" occur only in our English. The Hebrew usually does not identify the pronoun separately from the verb form itself.

(1) In this case, the verbs are just 3rd person singular which could be "*he,*" "*she,*" or "*it.*" In this case, since it refers back to DAVAR ("Word"), it is properly translated as "it." I might add that the first verb phrase, "*it shall not return*" (SHOOV) is IMPERFECT and the 2nd, 3rd, and 4th are PERFECT.

(2) "it shall accomplish" (ASAH),

(3) "It shall prosper" (TSALACH)

(4) "I sent it" (SHALACHTI) are all PERFECT.

(5) The 5th "it" in v. 13, "It shall be" is also PERFECT (HAYAH).

Since there are no pronouns used in any of these verbs, but are included in the verb form itself, and since they are all singular verbs, they can all be "*it*" without any problem. Whether the 5th "*it*" refers back to "Word" must rest solely on an interpretation, not on Hebrew grammar. Grammar doesn't tell you to what the "it" refers.. I believe you have every interpretive right to refer the 5th "*it*" back to "*Word*."

What else could be "to the LORD for a name, for an everlasting sign that shall not be cut off"? It is definitely singular, so it could not refer back to the people with their joy, or to the plural mountains or hills or trees or hands. It would seem strange for it to refer back to other singular words like joy, peace, field, thorn, brier, or tree. According to my way of interpreting the context, "*Word*" must be it to which the "it" is referring. I'm sure you concur.

"Files" in 1 Samuel 13:21

QUESTION #262

Please help me in this one:
1 Samuel 13:21 Yet they had a file (p@tsiyrah peh) for the mattocks, and for the coulters, and for the forks, and for the axes, and to sharpen the goads.
{A file: Heb. a file with mouths, or Heb. a pim, a third of a shekel} {sharpen: Heb. set} (KJV)
What does the KJV means when it says, They had "*a file*"?

Our Bible reads like the NKJV:
1 Samuel 13:21 and the charge for a sharpening was a pim for the plowshares, the mattocks, the forks, and the axes, and to set the points of the goads.

1 Samuel 13:21 Y el precio era un pim por las rejas de arado y por los azadones, por los tridentes, o las hachas; hasta para una aguijada que se hubiera de componer. (SRV04)

Looks to me that when it says they had a file, is it like a price list? Or a collection's storage, what was it? "Tarifa" Tariff, duty, tax,?

Also if I go to the dictionary and check file it also gives me the words, rub, polish, scrape, sand, sand paper, smooth.

How can I write it?

1 Samuel 13:21 Y tenían un _____ para las rejas de arado, para los azadones, para los tridentes, para las hachas, y para afilar las aguijadas.

(un folio, una tarifa, un lugar, un afilador,) I will appreciate your help, thanks.

ANSWER #262

My Hebrew lexicon says that the word PETZIRAH is "*uncertain.*" "*perhaps sharpening or bluntness*" according to two different Hebrew dictionaries. The next word, PIM, is from PEH which means "*mouth or end.*" If it is uncertain, what is to prevent us from siding with the KJB translators who must have had good reason to believe it was some sort of a "*file*" the "*end*" or PEH of which was to SHARPEN the various tools mentioned.

Where to these other versions like NKJV, NASV, and others get "PRICE" from PETZIRAH?? The root of this word is PETZAR which definitely means "*to press or to push.*" If this is the case, why not use a tool to press or to push or to FILE these tools to SHARPEN THEM? I'm afraid I side with the KJB translators on this one rather than on the other editors. It is only used once in the Old Testament and is therefore a *hapax legomenon*, as they call it (once written). With the KJB translators' knowledge of sister languages or cognate languages, they might have been using Aramaic, or Syriac, or Arabic or some other sister language to Hebrew to figure out this once-used word that the "scholars" of today know nothing about. What do they do with the word PIM which is from PEH or "*mouth or end*"? PEH comes from PAWAW which means "*to cleave in pieces.*" Perhaps that is what the "*file*" does. It cleaves a few pieces of dullness away from the dull mattocks, coulters, forks, etc. Verse 20 talks about "*sharpening*" the various implements. So verse 21 tells HOW they did this SHARPENING. It was with the END of an instrument called a FILE that did the SHARPENING. The context seems to bear out "FILE" or some other tool to SHARPEN these tools mentioned in v. 20.

Abel's Faithful Offering

QUESTION #263

Genesis 4:4 "*And Abel, he also brought of the firstlings of his flock and of the **fat thereof**. And the LORD had respect unto Abel and to his offering: 5 But unto Cain and to his offering he had not respect. And Cain was very wroth, and his countenance fell.*"

Is the "*fat thereof*" actually the fat animals of the flock? or the fat of the "*firstlings*"?

ANSWER #263

I believe this "*of the fat thereof*" refers to the "*firstlings.*" They are "*of his flock*" as a prepositional modifying phrase, but the "*fat*" was taken from the "*firstlings*" of that flock.

Eve's Creation From Adam's Rib

QUESTION #264

Genesis 2:21 "*And the LORD God caused a deep sleep to fall upon Adam and he slept: and he took one of his ribs, and closed up **the flesh** instead thereof;*"

What is "*the flesh*"? What is "*thereof*"?

ANSWER #264

I believe the understanding of this verse is that God removed one of Adam's ribs and then filled in the place where the rib was with flesh so that the wound was not noticed but was smooth. "*Thereof*" usually means "*of it.,*" In this case I think it means "*instead of the rib.*" He substituted flesh to take its place.

The Old Testament In Greek (LXX)

QUESTION #265

I recently heard a preacher say this in a sermon:
"*The Greek Septuagint was the Old Testament translated from Hebrew into Greek. This translation was available during the time that Jesus Christ performed His ministry on this earth. There is evidence that in some of Jesus' quotes of the Old Testament, He quoted this Greek translation of the Old Testament Scriptures.*"
Is this true? I thought I'd heard something about the Septuagint from the DBS meetings but I'm not sure..

ANSWER #265

There is no firm evidence that there was a complete B.C. Septuagint (LXX) that included Genesis through Malachi in the Old Testament. Most of the schools teach this and most preachers have been taught this (as I was at Dallas Theological Seminary). Though there is evidence that a few O.T. books were translated from Hebrew to Greek in B.C., the entire O.T. cannot be proved to be in existence until the 200's or 300's A.D. as the 5th column of Origen's *HEXAPLA* Bible. The Lord Jesus Christ did not quote the LXX. If the words are identical, the LXX that quoted from the New Testament. Dr. DiVietro has a paper on *DID JESUS CHRIST AND THE APOSTLES QUOTE FROM THE LXX*? He shows that this is a false claim.

The Freedom of Man's Will

QUESTION #266

Proverbs 21:1 says: "*The king's heart is in the hand of the LORD, as the rivers of water: he turneth it whithersoever he will.*" Why would he not "*turn the hearts*" of the men involved in the preservation of His Words?

ANSWER #266

Though God is sovereign, yet He also has given humanity their freedom of will either to obey Him, or to disobey Him. Eve and Adam chose to disobey Him as do multitudes of Bible translators all around the world. I am glad that the translators of the King James Bible, to the best of their abilities, chose to obey Him in their methods of translating the proper preserved Hebrew, Aramaic, and Greek Words.

Sarah--"Scolded" Or "Reproved"?
QUESTION #267
Genesis 20:16 says: "*And unto Sarah he* [Abimelech] *said, Behold, I have given thy brother a thousand pieces of silver: behold, he is to thee a covering of the eyes, unto all that are with thee, and with all other: thus **she was reproved**.*"

Was Sarah "*scolded*" by him or was she "*reproved*" for her innocence?

ANSWER #267
Here are the various meanings of "*reproved*" below. In Verse 5 Sarah said "*he is my brother.*" Perhaps Sarah was "*reproved, judged, rebuked, and corrected*" because of this lie in complicity with Abraham who also lied.

03198 yakach {yaw-kahh'}
a primitive root; TWOT - 865; v
AV - reprove 23, rebuke 12, correct 3, plead 3, reason 2, chasten 2,
  reprover + 0376 2, appointed 1, arguing 1, misc 9; 59
1) to prove, decide, judge, rebuke, reprove, correct, be right
  1a) (Hiphil)
    1a1) to decide, judge
    1a2) to adjudge, appoint
    1a3) to show to be right, prove
    1a4) to convince, convict
    1a5) to reprove, chide
    1a6) to correct, rebuke
  1b) (Hophal) to be chastened
  1c) (Niphal) to reason, reason together
  1d) (Hithp) to argue

The Translation of Genesis 1:1
QUESTION #268
Is there any lexical reason the New RSV has "*in the beginning when . . .*" Instead of "*in the beginning, God created. .?*" I do not especially have a problem with when, but "*in the beginning God created*" is specific and clear to me. Any assistance would be appreciated.

ANSWER #268
I find no grammatical reason to translate Genesis 1:1 other than "*in the beginning God created . . .*" The Hebrew order is: "in the beginning created God." The verb and subject are sometimes reversed in both Hebrew and Greek for emphasis. "*When*" does not appear nor is it even implied. It should not be used.

This Book Solves Bible Problems

QUESTION #269

If you compare 2 Chronicles 22:1-8 with 2nd Kings 8:25-29, the age of the king Ahaziah listed as either 42 years or 22 years. The Bible dictionaries say this is a copyist mistake. ISBE says it is an error. I can't accept this, especially the latter.

ANSWER #269

The KJB accurately translates the Hebrew text. Dr. Gerardus D. Bouw answers this by proving that there were two men named Ahaziah, one was 22 years old and the other 42 years old. This is from his book *THE BOOK OF BIBLE PROBLEMS*, pp. 112-116. This book is available from our Bible For Today ministry for a gift of **$15.00 + $5.00 S&H**.

What Is The TORAH?

QUESTION #270

I have had a question for awhile, and have tried to determine whether or not I should know the answer, given the materials on the Bible-text issue, but have determined that I need more input on this question. The question is this: Is the "Torah" the "Traditional Hebrew Masoretic Text?"

ANSWER #270

All TORAH refers to is to the first five books of Moses (Gen-Dt.). I suppose there might be different Hebrew editions used, but I think the official Hebrew would be the Traditional Hebrew Masoretic Text.

Hebrew & Greek Lexicons

QUESTION #271

What is your opinion of Dr. Merrill F. Unger, formerly a Professor of Hebrew at the Dallas Theological Seminary in Dallas, Texas? What interlinear and Hebrew and Greek lexicon do you recommend?

ANSWER #271

Dr. Unger was my teacher at Dallas Seminary in Hebrew and in other classes. He was a pleasant and kind teacher. However, like the other professors at Dallas Seminary, he would use the Critical Greek Text. He also made corrections in the Hebrew Old Testament Text in his Isaiah class.

Jay Green's Interlinear is helpful in finding the Hebrew and Greek words that are used; but, he uses his own translation in English rather than the KJB. George Ricker Berry's Interlinear is also helpful. After you find the Hebrew and Greek words used, I would recommend you get and use both the

ANALYTICAL HEBREW LEXICON and the ANALYTICAL GREEK LEXICON for the accurate meanings of those words. You can order these lexicons from our Bible For Today ministries.

"Pillows To All Amholes"

QUESTION #272

In Ezekiel 13:18, it is talking about *"women that sew pillows to all armholes, and make kerchiefs upon the head of every stature to hunt souls!"* What is meant here?

ANSWER #272

Ezekiel 13:18, as it reads in our KJB, seems to me to be referring to women prostitutes making it more comfortable for them to lie on their backs for sex with the pillows on their armholes. The colorful kerchiefs are to attract men to their houses. Though there might be other meanings, this is how I understand the meaning of this verse.

Greek & Hebrew Tenses

QUESTION #273

My pastor says that the Greek language has 110 tenses and that the Hebrew has 1100 tenses and that the latter all had to be memorized. Can you verify for me if this number of tenses is so? I find it hard to believe. The statement has been made several times and is not just a slip of the tongue.

ANSWER #273

There might be 110 forms of Greek words if you count the 3 singular forms and the 3 plural forms of all the tenses, including the masculine, feminine and neuter of the participles, and active and passive forms (I haven't counted them recently), but there are not 110 tenses as such. Perhaps he used the wrong word. Off the top of my head, in the Greek language, there are the present, imperfect, aorist, perfect, pluperfect tenses. Each of these has active forms, passive forms, and middle forms.

The same is true for the Hebrew tenses. There might be that many forms of the Hebrew words, including the 3 singular forms and 3 plural forms of the tenses. Off the top of my head again, there is the qal, qal perfect, qal imperfect, niphal, hiphil, piel, pual, hithpiel, hithpual tenses and active voice and passive voice forms. But there are not 100 tenses as such. Perhaps he was using a wrong term for these forms of the Hebrew.

Autographs And Apographs

QUESTION #274

What is an "*apograph*"? Would you please define that for me?

ANSWER #274

The word, "APOGRAPH" comes from two Greek words, APO ("*from*") and GRAPHO ("*to write*"). It is related to "AUTOGRAPH" which comes from AUTO ("*same*" or "*original*") and GRAPHO ("*to write*"). The autographs are the original writings of Hebrew, Aramaic, and Greek. The apographs are copies (hopefully exact copies) of those original Hebrew, Aramaic and Greek words.

The Use of ETH In Hebrew

QUESTION #275

I briefly spoke with Dr. D. A. Waite when he had finished speaking on Sunday evening in Newtownards, Northern Ireland. I asked a question regarding the meaning of the Hebrew word, ETH in Genesis 1:1. I was very pleased to get a proper answer. I would appreciate if it could be repeated in text form. I was hoping to pass on the reply to the person who suggested that ETH had a meaning which you explained clearly was not true.

ANSWER #275

The Hebrew form, ETH, is called a particle. It is made up of the two Hebrew letters, ALEPH and TAU. According to one Hebrew Lexicon, ETH is not translated in the King James Bible 22 times throughout the Old Testament. In the grammar of the Hebrew language, ETH is the "*sign of the definite direct object, not translated in English but generally preceding and indicating the accusative.*"

It occurs two times in Genesis 1:1. Once before "*heaven*" and once before "*earth*" because God created the "*heaven*" (a direct object of "*created*") and the "*earth*" (also a direct object of "*created*"). The ETH is very clearly merely a sign of the direct object in the Old Testament Hebrew Text.

Where Is "Paradise" Now?

QUESTION #276
Would you have time to explain some verses to me in 1st Samuel 28? Where was Samuel when he was down. I assumed that he went to Paradise when he died. Could you tell me where hell and Paradise were situated in relation to this earth. Did Saul and his sons go to paradise?

ANSWER #276
I do not believe Saul went to Paradise because of his unbelief. He seems to have been used of the Devil to destroy the Lord's anointed (David) through whom our Messiah would be born. I have no opinion about his sons, but I wonder about them. Those in Israel who, in faith, looked forward beyond the animal sacrifices to the Lamb of God Who would one day take away the sins of the world would be saved. Others would be lost. It appears that Sheol (the place of O.T. departed spirits) was under the earth's crust. It was divided into two sections, (1) the blessed section, and (2) the condemned section. Samuel was in the blessed section.

The Author Of The Pentateuch

QUESTION #277
Who is the true writer of the first five Bible books?

ANSWER #277
I believe that Moses is the Biblical and true author of the first five books of the Bible (Genesis through Deuteronomy). However, the modernist liberals have denied this because of their false concepts of *"higher criticism"* as it is called. They divide these five books into four sources. This false theory was devised by two apostate Germans called Graf and Wellhausen. It is called the "*documentary hypothesis*." They invented four false authors, J, E, P. and D.

The theory is not Biblical because the Lord Jesus quotes from all five of these books and attributes them all to Moses. I have copied below the true view so you can be prepared to meet this problem head on. You can share it with those who were asking about it too.

> **HERE IS THE TRUE AND BIBLICAL VIEW**
> **The Pentateuch**

While there is some disagreement between scholars over the authorship of the first five books of the Old Testament (The Pentateuch) it seems fairly obvious from internal sources that Moses was indeed the writer. Growing up in Pharaoh's house and being educated by the finest teachers in Egypt, Moses was well able to write (Acts 7:22). Throughout Scripture we come across confirmation to this end.

Evidence within the Pentateuch

The first five books continually refer to the fact that Moses wrote what God commanded him to so that he could read these words to the people, *"And the LORD said unto Moses, Write this for a memorial in a book, and rehearse it in the ears of Joshua"* (Exodus 17:14), *"And Moses wrote all the words of the LORD"* (Exodus 24:4), *"And the LORD said unto Moses, Write thou these words ..."* (Exodus 34:27), *"And Moses wrote their goings out according to their journeys by the commandment of the LORD"* (Numbers 33:2), *"Moses therefore wrote this song the same day, and taught it the children of Israel"* (Deuteronomy 31:22).

> These references prove that Moses wrote down exactly what God commanded him to write, but he also recorded details of the Israelites journeyings around the wilderness. He continued to write up until they entered into the Promised Land. The Pentateuch contains many more evidences that Moses was the author.

Evidence from other Old Testament Books

God spoke to Joshua and said, *"Only be thou strong and very courageous, that thou mayest observe to do according to all the law, which Moses my servant commanded thee ..."* (Joshua 1:7). Joshua not only remembered the words of Moses but he was able also to copy a record of the Law upon stone, *"He wrote there upon the stones a copy of the law of Moses, which he wrote in the presence of the children of Israel"* (Joshua 8:32). For Joshua to do this he must have had a written record of the law, also he ascribed the authorship of the law to Moses.

David charged his son Solomon as follows: *"keep the charge of the LORD thy God, to walk in his ways, to keep his statutes, and his commandments, and his judgments, and his testimonies, as it is written in the law of Moses, that thou mayest prosper in all that thou doest, and whithersoever thou turnest thyself."* (1 Kings 2:3).

In his prayer Daniel prayed over the failings of the people of Israel, saying, *"Yea, all Israel have transgressed thy law, even by departing, that they*

Questions on the Old Testament and Its Texts

might not obey thy voice; therefore the curse is poured upon us, and the oath that is written in the law of Moses the servant of God, because we have sinned against Him" (Daniel 9:11).

Ezra spoke about the burnt offerings that were commanded in *"the law of Moses, the man of God"* (Ezra 3:2), and later in 6:18 he refers to *"the book of Moses."* Nehemiah, who worked alongside Ezra in the rebuilding of Jerusalem, also remarks about *"the book of the law of Moses"* (Nehemiah 8:1)

The last book of the Old Testament also fittingly makes reference to the Pentateuch. In it Malachi calls it *"the law of Moses."*

Again, there is overwhelming proof inside the Old Testament for ascribing its first five books to Moses and that Moses actually put down in writing what we read there.

Evidence from the Lord Jesus Christ

There can be no greater source for proving the authorship of the Pentateuch than the Lord Jesus Christ Himself. If He believed and taught that Moses wrote these books then we do not really need further persuasion. Throughout His ministry Christ had ample opportunity to quash the idea that Moses actually wrote the law, but instead He reaffirms this belief. In fact He makes reference to all five books as being the work of Moses.

Genesis: In Matthew 19:1-9 Jesus makes reference to Adam and Eve being joined together as husband and wife exactly as Moses described.

Exodus: Jesus said, *"Now that the dead are raised, even as Moses showeth at the bush, when he calleth the Lord the God of Abraham, and the God of Isaac, and the God of Jacob."* (Luke 20:37 with Exodus 3:6).

In Mark 7:10 we find Jesus stating, *"For Moses said, Honour thy father and thy mother; and whoso curseth father or mother let him die the death"* (see Exodus 20:12 & 21:17).

Leviticus: *"See thou tell no man; but go thy way, show thyself to the priests, and offer the gift that Moses commanded, for a testimony unto them."* (Matthew 8:4 with Leviticus 14:3-4, 10)

Numbers: *"And as Moses lifted up the serpent in the wilderness, even so must the Son of man be lifted up"* (John 3:14 with Numbers 21:9).

Deuteronomy: Mark 7:10 (as above) with Deuteronomy 5:16.

One of the strongest statements of the Lord concerning the Mosaic authorship is found in John 5:45-47, where He says, *"Do not think that I will accuse you to the Father: there is one that accuseth you, even Moses, in whom ye trust. For had ye believed Moses, ye would have believed me: for he wrote of me. But if ye believe not his writings, how shall ye believe my words?"* There are a number of things that Moses wrote in reference to the Lord:

1: Genesis 3:15 - The coming of the one who would destroy the serpent.
2: Genesis 49:10 - The Coming of Shiloh, the Lawgiver, of Judah.
3: Deuteronomy 18 :15, 18 - The coming of the Prophet.

After His resurrection Jesus also speaks of the law as being of Moses, "*These are the words which I spake unto you, while I was yet with you, that all things must be fulfilled, which were written in the law of Moses, and in the prophets, and in the psalms, concerning me*" (Luke 24:44).

Evidence from other New Testament Sources

The Sadducees: "*Master, Moses wrote unto us ...*" (Mark 12:19).

The Apostle John: "*For the law was given by Moses, but grace and truth came by Jesus Christ*" (John 1:17). The Apostle Paul: "*For Moses describeth the righteousness which is of the law, That the man which doeth those things shall live by them*" (Romans 10:5 with Leviticus 18:5); "*For it is written in the law of Moses, Thou shalt not muzzle the mouth of the ox that treadeth out the corn.*" (1 Corinthian 9:9 with Deuteronomy 25:4).

Philip: "*We have found Him, of whom Moses in the law, and the prophets, did write, Jesus of Nazareth, the son of Joseph*" (John 1:45).

Luke: "*And when the days of her purification according to the law of Moses were accomplished ...*" (Luke 2:22).

There can be little doubt that the Bible writers themselves believed that Moses wrote the Pentateuch. It would be safer to stand on the side of the Lord Jesus Christ and His disciples and prophets than to accept the teachings and scepticism of men.

Christ In The Old Testament
QUESTION #278

I have a question for you. I met a lady at the hotel who's name is Laurie and she is Jewish. I have been talking to her a little about God but I can see the things she was taught and she wants to know more about what is truth. Where in the Old Testament does it talk about the Lord Jesus, besides Isaiah? I would like her to see that plus show her what God says in the New Testament also. I am praying that God will open her heart to the gospel. Any help would be most appreciated!

ANSWER #278

You'll never convince a Jew that Christ is prophesied in the Old Testament if they do not want to believe it, but at least we who are saved should know some of the OT foreshadowings of the Cross and Calvary. I think Isaiah 53 and

Psalm 22 are certainly the two clearest passages. Words from these two chapters are quoted in the NT as a fulfillment of them. But again, don't hold your breath about this Jewess lady finding Christ in the Old Testament. She must find Him in the clear teachings of the New Testament which are plain. She must realize she is a sinner like any Gentile, and come humbly to her Messiah/Christ and receive Him just like the Jews of the New Testament such as Paul, Peter, Andrew, Matthew, Luke, Thomas, James, and the others.

I am attaching these two chapters in PDF so you can see the various verses that apply.

"Rock" As A Name For "God"
QUESTION #279
Which Hebrew Masoretic Text has the phrase: "*there is no God, I know not any*"? Isaiah 44:8, in some versions has "*is there any other Rock*"?
ANSWER #279
The Hebrew Masoretic Words underlying the King James Bible has this clause in Isaiah 44:8. The word, "*Rock*," is one of the Names of God in the O.T. and was thus properly interpreted as "*God*" by the KJB translators in Isaiah 44:8. "*Rock*" is a noun describing the Lord in many verses (Cf. Psalm 18:2; 18:31, 46; 28:1; 31:3; 42:9;62:2;, 6; 71:3; and especially 1 Cor. 10:4 where that "*Rock*" was the Lord Jesus Christ Himself.

Origin Of The Hebrew Vowel Points
QUESTION #280
What about the Hebrew vowel points. Have they always been used?
ANSWER #280
The Hebrew vowel points were from the very beginning of God's creation of man and of the writing of the Bible. Sometimes modern Hebrew does not use the vowel points. Without the vowels, the consonants do not make distinct words. God gave us Words. Consonants alone can make several different words if different vowels are used. There would be no inerrancy in the Hebrew OT unless vowels were there originally. The authority on this is Dr. Thomas Strouse. He has two excellent articles regarding the Hebrew vowel points which we carry.

Meaning of "Seek The Lord"

QUESTION #281

What does it mean to "*seek the Lord*" in Amos 5:6 and in other verses in the Bible?

ANSWER #281

"*Seek the Lord*" is found 27 times in our King James Bible. It is only once in the N.T. and 26 in the O.T. Here are some of the various meanings of DARASH in the Hebrew O.T.

01875 darash {daw-rash'}
a primitive root; TWOT - 455; v
AV - seek 84, enquire 43, require 12, search 7, misc 18; 164
1) to resort to, seek, seek with care, enquire, require
  1a) (Qal)
    1a1) to resort to, frequent (a place), (tread a place)
    1a2) to consult, enquire of, seek
      1a2a) of God
      1a2b) of heathen gods, necromancers
    1a3) to seek deity in prayer and worship
      1a3a) God
      1a3b) heathen deities
    1a4) to seek (with a demand), demand, require
    1a5) to investigate, enquire
    1a6) to ask for, require, demand
    1a7) to practice, study, follow, seek with application
    1a8) to seek with care, care for
  1b) (Niphal)
    1b1) to allow oneself to be enquired of, consulted (only of God)
    1b2) to be sought, be sought out
    1b3) to be required (of blood)

I hope this helps you to understand the meaning of "*seeking the Lord.*"

Differences Of "Soul" & "Spirit"

QUESTION #282

Would it be acceptable to use the words "*soul*" and "*spirit*" interchangeably? Is the "*soul*" that's mentioned in 1 Kings 17:21-22 the same part of man as the "*spirit*" mentioned in Luke 8:55?

1 Kings 17:21-22 reads:

> "*And he stretched himself upon the child three times, and cried unto the LORD, and said, O LORD my God, I pray thee, let this child's **soul** come into him again. And the LORD heard the voice of Elijah;*

and the **soul** *of the child came into him again, and he revived."*
Luke 8:55 reads:
*"And her **spirit** came again, and she arose straightway: and he commanded to give her meat."*

ANSWER #282

I do not believe "*spirit*" and "*soul*" should be combined. 1 Thessalonians 5:23 is clear that there is a distinction and it should not be united and blended together.

1 Thessalonians 5:23 reads:
"And the very God of peace sanctify you wholly; and I pray God your whole spirit and soul and body be preserved blameless unto the coming of our Lord Jesus Christ."

The Greek word PNEUMA ("*spirit*") and PSYCHE ("*soul*") are separate words. In the Hebrew, RUACH ("*spirit*") and NEPHESH ("*soul*") are also separate words and should not be confused.

It is true that both spirit and soul are part of man's immaterial nature. From that standpoint, they are in the same category. But they must be defined and expounded separately. This is a subject in itself. If indeed, you believe that the words "*spirit*" and "*soul*" are identical, you could refer to "*God the Holy Spirit*" also as "*God the Holy Soul.*" I believe this would be blasphemy.

What Is A "Leviathan"?

QUESTION #283
What is a behemoth and a leviathan?

ANSWER #283
It is not certain what these two creatures are. Here is what the *Wikipedia* says about them as mentioned in the book of Job.

"Behemoth and Leviathan are listed alongside a number of other animals that are clearly mundane, such as goats, eagles, and hawks, leading some Christian scholars to surmise that Behemoth and Leviathan may also be mundane creatures. Some propose Leviathan was a <u>Nile crocodile</u>. Like the Leviathan, the Nile crocodile is aquatic, scaly, and possesses fierce teeth. Job 41:18 states that Leviathan's eyes "are like the eyelids of the morning." Others suggest that the Leviathan is an exaggerated account of a <u>whale</u>. However, Job also goes on to describe Leviathan as 'breathing fire.'"

"Some <u>Young Earth Creationists</u> have alleged that Leviathan was

either a dinosaur, such as <u>Parasaurolophus</u> (despite being a herbivore and a non-aquatic animal), or a giant marine reptile, such as <u>Kronosaurus</u> (despite lacking armor and a serpentine body).[4] Other Young Earth Creationists say that the giant <u>crocodilian, Sarcosuchus,</u> best fits the description in the Bible.[5]

"Heaven" Or "Heavens"?

QUESTION #284

Why did the King James Bible translators translate "*heaven*" in the singular in Genesis 1:1 but make it plural in 2:1.

ANSWER 284

I don't know what was behind this, other than taking the "*heaven*" as a collective to be parallel with earth (ARETZ) which is a singular. It could also be taken as a "plural of majesty" which emphasizes something great and majestic yet it is plural with a singular translation. The context determines whether this plural term is translated as to a singular collective, or a plural.

What Is "Sheol"?

QUESTION #285

Does the Traditional Hebrew Masoretic Text contain the word "SHEOL" in the following references as is indicated below?

If so, then is it your opinion that the KJV mistranslates these references?

The references below come from the Jehovah's Witnesses *New World Translation* which I find extremely suspect of virtually everything in it; thus, the question.

<u>The Sixty-Six Occurrences of Sheol</u>

SHEOL occurs 66 times in the New World Translation of the Hebrew Scriptures, namely, in Ge 37:35; 42:38; 44:29, 31; Nu 16:30, 33; De 32:22; 1Sa 2:6; 2Sa 22:6; 1Ki 2:6, 9; Job 7:9; 11:8; 14:13; 17:13, 16; 21:13; 24:19; 26:6; Ps 6:5; 9:17; 16:10; 18:5; 30:3; 31:17; 49:14, 14, 15; 55:15; 86:13; 88:3; 89:48; 116:3; 139:8; 141:7; Pr 1:12; 5:5; 7:27; 9:18; 15:11, 24; 23:14; 27:20; 30:16; Ec 9:10; Ca 8:6; Isa 5:14; 7:11; 14:9, 11, 15; 28:15, 18; 38:10, 18; 57:9; Eze 31:15, 16, 17; 32:21, 27; Ho 13:14, 14; Am 9:2; Jon 2:2; Hab 2:5.

Questions on the Old Testament and Its Texts

ANSWER #285
I checked the first two references and SHEOL is in the Hebrew. I would expect that all your references would have SHEOL as well without checking. The difference between the KJB and the NWT is that the NWT does not translate SHEOL, but only transliterates. The KJB actually translates this word in various ways.

Two Versions On Genesis 27:39-40
QUESTION #286
I wondered if you would explain if there is a difference in what is being said in these two bible versions. I'm looking at Genesis 27:39-40. It seems like the KJB is saying something different from the NASB concerning Esau.

King James Bible: *"And Isaac his father answered and said unto him, Behold, thy dwelling shall be the fatness of the earth, and of the dew of heaven from above;"*

NASB: *"Then Isaac his father answered and said to him, 'Behold, away from the fertility of the earth shall be your dwelling, And away from the dew of heaven from above.'"*

In the KJB, it seems to be that his dwelling is in the best portions (fatness) with the dew of heaven but in the NASV it seems that it is "*away*" from that (fertility of earth and dew). Are two different things being said?

ANSWER #286
These two translations are opposite, as you point out. The NASV seems to make the "MEM" as "*from or away from*" rather than part of the noun, MASHMAN which itself means "*fatness*" and not "*from or away from fatness or fertility.*"

Don't Trust The Dead Sea Scrolls
QUESTION #287
I am curious about the Dead Sea Scrolls. Various articles have pointed out differences between them and the Hebrew text. Should we trust them or the Masoretic Hebrew Words underlying the King James Bible?

ANSWER #287
The articles and Bible versions that favor the Dead Sea Scrolls are mostly from liberal skeptics or Bible-believing people who deny that God has preserved His Hebrew, Aramaic, and Greek Words underlying our KJB. I think it is wisest for you not to be influenced by them. They will lead you astray and bring "*leanness to your soul*" (Psalm 106:15). For those who take the time to research it, there is a satisfactory explanation for every one of the critics'

> objections to the O.T. Hebrew or Aramaic Words underlying the KJB. There is no end to the thousands and thousands of the critics' objections, and it is wisest to "*let them alone*" as the Lord advised His disciples concerning the Pharisees in Matthew 15:14:

"*Let them alone: they be blind leaders of the blind. And if the blind lead the blind, both shall fall into the ditch.*"

I would advise you not to pursue the Dead Sea Scrolls (DSS) any further. You have enough to confuse you. They are worthless from the standpoint of truth and are used to confuse the saints. I believe they are one of Satan's masterpieces in his role as an "*angel of light*" (2 Corinthians 11:14)

There are various questions I have concerning the Dead Sea Scrolls: (1) We don't know if the Essenes had an authentic copy of the O.T. Hebrew from which to copy. (2) We do not know their technique of copying, whether good or bad.

Yearly Bible Reading-How?

QUESTION #288

Today and yesterday I started reading through 2 Kings and 2 Chronicles again. I moved from Revelation to Zechariah, then decided I needed to refresh my memory about the kings in Israel and Judah. I'm sure I'll have more questions as I continue reading. Do you any suggestions on Bible reading?

ANSWER #288

You might begin with our daily Bible reading from Genesis through Revelation verse by verse, 85 verses per day. You click on the LINK below for it. (http://www.biblefortoday.org/idx_bible_reading.htm) if you wish. It only takes from 10 to 15 minutes/daily. You can also hear the brief eight to ten minutes of comments on these verses from Genesis through Revelation each day at

(http://www.biblefortoday.org/BibleSermons/bible_comments.htm) if you wish. This might give you a grasp of the entire Bible in one year in brief fashion and then you could study further in other areas of interest as well.

The Recommended Hebrew Text

QUESTION #289
What published Hebrew text do you recommend?

ANSWER #289
I have been recommending and carrying the Hebrew Letteris Text of 1866 referred to in the e-mail. It is published by the British and Foreign Bible Society. We have been getting it from the American Bible Society. Since it was published in 1866, it came out well before the days when they began to tamper with the Masoretic Hebrew Words. This is why I believe it to be the Hebrew underlying our King James Bible, the Daniel Bomberg edition of 1524-1525. This text was used for 400 years and even by Rudolf Kittel in his 1906 and 1912 editions. His edition was changed in the 1937 edition

<u>I don't trust the BIBLIA HEBRAICA of either Kittel or Stuttgartensia though both are in print and available.</u> The Hebrew woman used by the Trinitarian Bible Society (Dr. Anderson) thinks there is very little difference between this text and Ben Chayyim, but that is her opinion. I have been trying to get some people to scan the Letteris Text, put it into computer format, and then compare it with the Stuttgartensia or Kittel editions. One man began it but has stopped. He at first told me there were many changes even in Genesis. Here is one of my Power Point slides I use when talking about the Hebrew text.

THE TWO HEBREW TEXTS
1. TRUE TEXT
Traditional Masoretic Text
Daniel Bomberg Edition
2nd Great Rabbinic Bible
Edited by Ben Chayyim (1524-25 A.D.)
The Unquestioned Hebrew Text
For the Next 400 Years
Used in Kittel's 1906 & 1912
BIBLIA HEBRAICA
Used in our KING JAMES BIBLE

2. FALSE TEXT
An Abridged Masoretic Text
From only ONE Hebrew Manuscript
Leningrad Manuscript (B19a or "L")
(1008 A.D.)
Edited by Ben Asher

Used in Kittel's 1937 Edition
BIBLIA HEBRAICA
And the STUTTGARTENSIA Edition
c. 20,000--30, 000 Footnote Suggested Changes to the Text
Used in ALL Modern Versions

Who Was Melchisedec?

QUESTION #290

I don't understand about Melchisedec having neither beginning nor end. What does Hebrews 7:3 mean when it says:

"*Without father, without mother, without* `, **having neither beginning of days, nor end of life**; *but made like unto the Son of God; abideth a priest continually.*")

What does it mean to have "*no beginning of days*"?

ANSWER #290

To begin with, the Hebrew name, Melchisedec, means "*king*" (melech) of "*righteousness*" (tsadiq)." In brief, I believe Melchisedec was what is known as a Theophany ("*an appearance of God*") or a Christophany ("*an appearance of Christ*") in the Old Testament in His pre-incarnate state. As such, He was "*without father, without mother, without descent.*" This was a prefiguring of Christ's eternal High Priesthood. In other words he was a type of the Lord Jesus Christ Himself. This view is held by many Bible teachers. The 9 references to him in Hebrews 5, 6, and 7 do not contradict this understanding.

Hebrew Versus Septuagint (LXX)

QUESTION #291

Hebrews 1:6 makes reference to ". . . *let all the angels of God worship him.*"

The cross reference is to Deuteronomy 32:43 It isn't in the KJB OT, but in the LXX. What is the explanation that the Masoretic Text doesn't have this phrase?

ANSWER #291

I would just say that it was a fact that the Lord said, "*let all the angels of God worship Him.*" God would not necessarily have to be quoting Scripture. I believe the LXX (which cannot be trusted for anything) added this phrase from Hebrews 1:6. This was possible because, as I believe, the LXX appeared in the 200's A.D. in Origin's day. Hebrews 1:6 was available for the LXX to copy.

Questions on the Old Testament and Its Texts

Understanding Proverbs 18:24

QUESTION #292

I am writing in hope that you would give me your thoughts on Proverbs 18:24. This verse was brought up to me by an individual as we were discussing the King James against other translations. In doing some word studies on the verse, I found that there seemed to be some validity to his position of accepting Darby's translation of that verse. I believe that I have settled in my mind that the King James translators got it right. Would you please comment on this verse.

Darby's Translation of Proverbs 18:24

"*A man of many friends will come to ruin but there is a friend that sticketh closer than a brother.*"

King James Bible of Proverbs 18:24

"*A man that hath friends must shew himself friendly: and there is a friend that sticketh closer than a brother.*"

ANSWER #292

The answer to this is that RESH AYIN (The "R" and the "Y" in Hebrew) are the two Hebrew letters in both "*friend*" and in "*evil.*" It depends on the vowels underneath these consonants that make the difference in the meaning.

The KJB and NKJV men took the verb as meaning "*friend*" and the NASV, NIV and Darby took it as "*evil.*" This is perhaps the reason for these differences. I see no reason to doubt the King James Bible's Hebrew text.

Need A Sound Arabic Translation

QUESTION #293

Do you know if there is a good Arabic translation of the Bible? One that can be used for those that only read Arabic?

ANSWER #293

The best man to tell you about this would be Pastor Darrell Sutton. He has mastered Hebrew and Arabic and I think he would know of a good Arabic translation if there is one. His e-mail is pastordarrell@tgarc.org if you would like to write him.

The Competing N.T. Greek Texts

QUESTION #294

1. How many camps are there that resist the Critical Greek Text?
2. What are the differences between the Critical Greek Text and the Textus Receptus Text of Scrivener?
3. Are these differences important doctrinally?

4. Is there anywhere these doctrinal passages are specified?

ANSWER #294

1. The two groups against the Gnostic Critical Greek Text are (1) the so-called "*Majority*" or "*Byzantine Text*," and (2) those who follow the Textus Receptus or Received Text. I favor this group..

2. The textual differences between the TR of Dr. Scrivener that underlies the KJB and the Nestle/Aland 26 or 27 total 8,000 places. These are specified in Dr. Jack Moorman's book, *8,000 Differences Between the Critical Text and the Textus Receptus* (**BFT #3084 @ $20.00 + $5.00 S&H**)..

3. As far as the doctrinal importance of these 8,000 differences, there are a total of 356 doctrinal passages that are found in these 8,000 differences. This is a serious problem that is found in all the modern versions in any language in the world that is based on this Gnostic Critical Greek Text.

4. These 356 doctrinal passages are specified by Dr. Jack Moorman in his book, *Early Manuscripts, Church Fathers, and the Authorized Version* (**BFT #3230 @ $20.00 + $5.00 S&H**). The so-called "Majority Text" is a separate subject with many problems, but not as many as the Gnostic Critical Text.

CHAPTER III
MISCELLANEOUS QUESTIONS

Verses Against Drinking Alcohol

QUESTION #295

I was wondering if there are examples of actions or behaviors that the Bible doesn't specifically say "*Thou shalt not*" to, but that are plainly understood that we are not to do. The reason I was thinking about this is for someone who says, "*There's no command in the Bible saying, Thou shalt not drink alcohol.*" Although Proverbs 23:31 seems like a pretty clear commandment to me.

ANSWER #295

There might not be clear commands in the Bible about certain things, but there are principles which we can apply.

For example, 1 Corinthians 10:31 "*Whether therefore ye eat, or drink, or whatsoever ye do, do all to the glory of God.*"

Also 1 John 2:15-17 "*Love not the world, neither the things that are in the world. If any man love the world, the love of the Father is not in him. 16 For all that is in the world, the lust of the flesh, and the lust of the eyes, and the pride of life, is not of the Father, but is of the world. 17 And the world passeth away, and the lust thereof: but he that doeth the will of God abideth for ever.*"

Also Romans 12:1-2 "*I beseech you therefore, brethren, by the mercies of God, that ye present your bodies a living sacrifice, holy, acceptable unto God, which is your reasonable service. 2 And be not conformed to this world: but be ye transformed by the renewing of your mind, that ye may prove what is that good, and acceptable, and perfect, will of God.*"

Also 1 Corinthians 6:12 "*All things are lawful unto me, but all things are not expedient: all things are lawful for me, but I will not be brought under the power of any.*"

Also 1 Corinthians 9:27 "*But I keep under my body, and bring it into *subjection: lest that by any means, when I have preached to others, I myself should be a castaway."*

> In the area of drinking, the Greek word NEPHO means an *"absence of alcohol."* It is used for pastors, deacons, and other Christians in the following verses.

Here are a few verses that use either NEPHO or NEPHALIOS. The **bold** and underlined words represent these Greek words.

1 Thessalonians 5:6
 6 *"Therefore let us not sleep, as do others; but let us watch and be **sober**."* (KJV)

1 Thessalonians 5:8
 8 *"But let us, who are of the day, be **sober**, putting on the breastplate of faith and love; and for an helmet, the hope of salvation."* (KJV)

1 Timothy 3:2
 2 *"A bishop then must be blameless, the husband of one wife, **vigilant**, sober, of good behaviour, given to hospitality, apt to teach;"* (KJV)

1 Timothy 3:11
 11 *"Even so must their wives be grave, not slanderers, **sober**, faithful in all things."* (KJV)

2 Timothy 4:5
 5 *"But **watch** thou in all things, endure afflictions, do the work of an evangelist, make full proof of thy ministry."* (KJV)

Titus 2:2
 2 *"That the aged men be **sober**, grave, temperate, sound in faith, in charity, in patience."* (KJV)

1 Peter 1:13
 13 *"Wherefore gird up the loins of your mind, be **sober**, and hope to the end for the grace that is to be brought unto you at the revelation of Jesus Christ;"* (KJV)

3524 nephaleos {nayfal'ehos} or nephalios {nayfal'eeos}
from 3525; TDNT - 4:939,633; adj
AV - sober 2, vigilant 1; 3
1) sober, temperate
  1a) **abstaining from wine**
  1b) **of things free from all wine, as vessels, offerings**

Miscellaneous Questions

Will Babies Go To Heaven?

QUESTION #296

I didn't quite understand what a recent pastor was talking about the spiritual condition of babies and those whose minds are without the ability to understand the gospel. Do they go to heaven? Can you give a brief answer? I am just concerned about the condition of one of my relatives.

ANSWER #296

I believe the Bible implies that those who are mentally retarded like small babies who cannot think or decide to repent and receive the Lord Jesus Christ as Saviour, should they die in this state, they are protected from going to hell and are considered to be "*safe*" though not "*saved*." The basis of this is the following verses:
Matthew 18:10

"*Take heed that ye despise not one of **these little ones**; for I say unto you, That **in heaven their angels do always behold the face of my Father which is in heaven**.*" and other verses as well, such as:
2 Samuel 12:22-23

22 "*And he said, **While the child was yet alive**, I fasted and wept: for I said, Who can tell whether GOD will be gracious to me, that the child may live?*"

23 "*But now he is dead, wherefore should I fast? can I bring him back again? **I shall go to him, but he shall not return to me**.*"

This is not as clear a doctrine as others in the Bible, but it is generally held by Bible-believing Christians.

Seven Hills & Mark Of The Beast

QUESTION #297

I have heard teachings that the seven mountains are referring to the seven hills of Rome yet I wonder about that when looking at the context.

I also, wondered about the mark of the beast. The Bible says it is a mark "*in their right hand, or in their foreheads.*"

ANSWER #297

I agree that the great whore does refer to the seven hills of Rome. I believe Rome will be the leading role in the joining of all apostate religions of the earth, including Catholic, Protestant, Jewish, Islamic, Buddhist, Shintoist, Taoist, Christian Science, Jehovah Witnesses, Humanists, Scientologists, and on and on. The computer chips make the "*mark*" quite acceptable and understandable.

The Holy Spirit's Ministries
QUESTION #298

1. 1 Corinthians 12:13 says:"*For by one Spirit we are all baptized into one body.*" What does this mean?
2. What is the difference between water baptism and baptism of the Spirit?
3. You mentioned that the Holy Spirit has 5 ministries to the unsaved. Could you tell me what they are and the Bible verses that talk about these ministries?
4. You also named the 5 ministries of the Holy Spirit to the saved. Could you tell me what they are and the Bible verses that talk about these ministries?
5. You also mentioned the three "nots": "*grieve not the Spirit of God*," "*quench not the Spirit of God.*" What was the third requirement for the filling of the Holy Spirit?
6. I have a Christian friend who is made fun of by others in her church because she is physically unattractive and not smart. Even the pastor isn't friendly to her. In fact, one time, someone in her church gave her a recipe for making a single batch of cookies requiring 0.186 g margarine, 0.382 g sugar, 0.092g eggs, 0.558 g pumpkin filling, etc.! I then explained to my friend that that person was playing a cruel joke on her.

(I Corinthians 12:25 teaches "That there should be no schism in the body, but that the members should have the same care one for another.") How can I help my friend?

ANSWER #298

I'll answer by number below:
1. It means that upon salvation, every Christian is baptized by the Holy Spirit into one body and is joined to the Head (Christ) and all the other saved people (the members).
2. Baptism of the Spirit occurs upon salvation. Baptism in water occurs at some time later.
3. There are only two ministries to the unsaved, not seven:
   (1) reproving of sin (John 16:8)
   (2) restraining sin (2 Thessalonians 2:7) ("*letteth*" means "*restrains.*")
4. There are five ministries to the saved:
   (1) baptism (1 Corinthians 12:13)
   (2) regeneration (John 3:5)
   (3) indwelling (Romans 8:11; 1 Corinthians 3:16; 2 Timothy 1:14; James 4:5)
   (4) sealing (2 Corinthians 1:22; Ephesians 1:13; Ephesians 4:30;)
   (5) filling (Ephesians 5:18)
5. The third requirement for the filling of the Holy Spirit was positive: "*walk in the Spirit*" (Galatians 5:16 and 5:25)

6. You can speak with her on the phone and encourage her. You can be sure she is saved. You can take her out to lunch. You can invite her to your home for lunch and for visiting with her. You can pray for her.

Tongues And Other Spiritual Gifts

QUESTION #299

I have some questions to ask with regard to the recent Bible study on I Corinthians 12:1-10.
1. When was the Bible completed?
2. When the Bible was completed, which spiritual gifts ceased?
3. Are there Bible verses to show that these spiritual gifts ceased?
4. Why did the Christians in the New Testament times need these spiritual gifts which we do not need now?
5. Does God still perform physical healing?
6. Does God still perform miracles?
7. Do we consider Pentecostals and Charismatics our brethren in Christ or not? If so, why? If not, why not?
8. Why do we believe that "*tongues*" does not refer to an unintelligible language but rather refers to different languages spoken by people?
9. Why do Pentecostals and Charismatics believe that "*tongues*" refer to a language that is unintelligible?
10. Does God decide which spiritual gift to give to Christians or can a Christian ask God for a specific spiritual gift?
11. How does a Christian know what spiritual gift he has?

ANSWER #299

The answer is numbered below corresponding to the question above:
1. Between A.D. 90 and 100.
2. I believe there were nine special sign gifts that ceased: I'll list them here: 1. The special sign gift of tongues; 2. The special sign gift of interpretation of tongues; 3. The special sign gift of prophesy; 4. The special sign gift of word of wisdom; 5. The special sign gift of word of knowledge; 6. The special sign gift of healing; 7. The special sign gift of special faith; 8. The special sign gift of miracles; and 9. The special sign gift of special discerning of spirits.
3. 1 Corinthians 13:8 indicates 3 that have ceased upon the completion of the NT (when that which is perfect is come) and the others are implied, but there are no specifics on the other 6.
4. They needed them because the Bible was not completed (knowledge, prophecy, etc.). They were for special signs of proofs that the Christian faith was real.
5. When He wants to, yes, but not by specialized "healers."

6. When He wants to, yes, but not by specialized "miracle workers." The miracle of salvation is one.
7. Yes, if they are born-again.
8. Because GLOSSA means "*languages*."
9. Because of their different interpretations of 1 Corinthians 14.
10. The Lord gives spiritual gifts to Christians that He prepares to receive them.
11. The Lord reveals this to him or her as they live for the Lord Jesus Christ.

Yearly Bible Reading Schedule
QUESTION #300
I listened to part of the Daily OT Bible Reading # 9 earlier this morning and will probably listen to the rest of it later today. What made you choose the amount of 85 verses per day? Is it that if one reads 85 verses per day beginning on January 1st and starts from Genesis 1: 1, one will have read through the entire Word of God in exactly one year?

ANSWER #300
This is correct. If you divide the approximately 31,101 verses in the Bible by 365, you get on the average 85 verses per day. A few days, I make it 86 verses in order to come out properly. The schedule of Bible reading can be found on our BibleFortoday.org website.

What Is A "Separated" Church?
QUESTION #301
I believe your church is "*separated.*" Agreeing with that philosophy, I'd like to know in what ways your church is "*separated.*" I'd also like to know your position on "*soul-winning.*" How much emphasis should be placed on it in the local church? Is it the sole or main purpose of the local church? Is it the job of every Christian or is it the job of the church body, working together, fulfilling various points of the "*great commission*" ?

ANSWER #301
Yes, our Bible For Today Baptist Church is a "*separated church.*"
I am for it in a responsible manner, rather than a quick-prayerism, and no follow-up manner which is not Biblical.
The believers should be trained in the Bible as to verses to be used and how to use them in this duty. 2 Timothy 3:16--4:2 gives the emphasis of the Bible for each believer and on the preachers in preaching and teaching that Bible. This must be the primary emphasis of the local church. Because of this, I preach and teach verse-by-verse as I have done on www.BibleForToday.org

Miscellaneous Questions

(clicking on the **BROWN BOX**) from Romans through Revelation. When soul-winning is brought up, I preach on it.

> The Great Commission emphasizes the balance between soul-winning and "*teaching them to observe whatsoever*" Christ has "*commanded*" them. Evangelism must be accompanied with "*teaching to observe all things.*"

Matthew 28:19-20 says: "*Go ye therefore, and teach all nations, baptizing them in the name of the Father, and of the Son, and of the Holy Ghost: Teaching them to observe all things whatsoever I have commanded you.*"

It is the job of every Christian and of the church body to fulfill the great commission through tracts, personal witness, missions, TV, radio, and Internet ministry when possible.

Bible Interpretation Methods
QUESTION #302

I came across something that makes no sense to me so thought you could clarify. This is in regard to Bible interpretation. It was a ministry that says they are rediscovering the scriptures as Hebraic literature (as opposed to Hellenistic literature), demanding the hermeneutic models of Second Temple Period Judaism as a basis in biblical interpretation. I have absolutely no idea what that explanation means. In Christ,

> ### ANSWER #302
> Though I do not understand this fully, I would oppose using any method of Bible interpretation other than the "*conventional grammatical-historical model of interpretation.*" I don't trust the "*Second Temple Period Judaism*" or any other means of interpreting the Bible apart from the above method and the leading of God the Holy Spirit. The unsaved Jews do not have God the Holy Spirit indwelling them, so have zero opportunities for proper interpretation of the Bible. The "*natural man*" can't understand it. (1 Corinthians 2:14).

Numbers Seven & Three
QUESTION #303

I am trying to find out the meaning of why the Lord God uses the number seven and the number three in the Bible.

ANSWER #303

The Bible does not say number seven represents perfection. Neither does it give us any information about the meaning of number three. There are many who speculate on these numbers, but I do not believe we should go beyond what is written in the Bible. If meanings are assigned to any numbers, we should understand and agree that this is pure speculation rather than dogmatic Biblical truth.

Biblical Preservation And Writers
QUESTION #304
Bible preservation is the idea that God has kept His Words intact from generation to generation. Can a Biblical writer choose to vary the words of the Holy Spirit? If so, is he not adding or subtracting from what God said?

ANSWER 304
"*Biblical writers*" never chose any of the Hebrew, Aramaic, or Greek Words that they wrote. Every Word was chosen by God the Holy Spirit Who, in turn, received those Words from the Lord Jesus Christ. If there seems to be a variation in wording anywhere in the Bible, it was not the "*Biblical writer*" who varied it, but God the Holy Spirit and God the Son who did so. And we must never question these variations that God, for His own reasons and purposes, has set forth in the Bible.

God's Gift And Christmas Gifts
QUESTION #305
I thought that I might put a few thoughts of my own your way concerning Christmas. Am I just being an Old Scrooge now that I am grown up? Is it truly possible to include Jesus and trees and gifts into Christmas and not make a mockery of what God has done for us in bringing his Son to die for us? So, what is the answer? Can one be justified in doing what my parents did? Is it possible to do as the wise men did with our kids as a symbol of how they are loved, as evidently the Son of God was loved by these wise men, that they would bestow great gifts on Jesus?

ANSWER #305
I believe that each of us must make up his or her mind about this day for themselves, whether to accept the day with all of its pagan origins or to reject it. It is true that we must never forget the Incarnation of God the Son Who became perfect Man, but the entire Christmas emphasis has no bearing whatever on that miraculous event. It is sad that we have to tie a make-believe Santa and all of the other things in with that blessed miraculous event.

Miscellaneous Questions 69

Pulpit Attacks & Gail Riplinger

QUESTION #306

I've got a couple of things to run by you if you have the time.

(1) The pastor of the church where some KJB people were members attacked them from the pulpit. What should they do?

(2) What do you think of Gail Riplinger? I'm reluctant to hand out *New Age Bible Versions* to people until this possibly gets cleared up in my mind. I would appreciate your thoughts.

ANSWER #306

(1) When a pastor attacks your position on the King James Bible and its underlying Hebrew, Aramaic, and Greek Words, I believe it is time to leave that church.

(2) I must admit that at first, I sided with Gail Riplinger against David Cloud in his analysis of Riplinger's *New Age Bible Versions* (NABV). Having found serious defects in the character of Gail Riplinger which I had not known about, I have since apologized to David Cloud and have been given his critique of the NABV. His research should be listened to carefully. Mrs. Waite and I have changed our opinion about Gail Riplinger in recent years.

I have recently written a book about Gail Riplinger. If you want to get a free PDF copy of this book, write an E-mail to BFT@BibleForToday.org requesting it and I'll send it to you without charge. Or, you can get a copy of this 134-page book as follows: *A WARNING!! On Gail Riplinger's KJB & Multiple Inspiration HERESY* (BFT #3464 @ $15.00 + $5.00 S&H).

What Is "Vision Forum"?

QUESTION #307

I've not heard of the Vision Forum Movement. What is it?

ANSWER #307

Here is a link about Vision Forum which you can follow. Basically it urges to have house churches and takes a very strong, though erroneous, stand on hyper-Calvinist theology. We are listed as a house church with them because we're a house church, not because we're with them in their heresy of hyper-Calvinism. We've had several references from people who are with them and when they find we're not hyper-Calvinist, they shy away. We had one large family do this. Below is a LINK to Vision Forum.

http://search.netscape.com/ns/boomframe.jsp?query=vision+forum&page=1
&offset=0&result_url=redir%3Fsrc%3Dwebsearch%26requestId%3De0777
82b57f4299a%26clickedItemRank%3D10%26userQuery%3Dvision%2Bfor
um%26clickedItemURN%3Dhttp%253A%252F%252Fen.wikipedia.org%2

52Fwiki%252FVision_Forum%26invocationType%3D-%26fromPage%3D
NSCPToolbarNS%26amp%3BampTest%3D1&remove_url=http%3A%2F%
2Fen.wikipedia.org%2Fwiki%2FVision_Forum

N.T. Elders And House Churches

QUESTION #308

I have a Bible study called Bible History and Geography from David Cloud's ministry. I came to a section of which I have a question, as it seems like a different teaching than what I've had from you, or perhaps I'm not understanding the teaching from the book. I'll type up the section in question:

They organized the churches (Acts 14:23)

Section (b) is where I have a question, page 176:

(b) Elders are required for a proper New Testament church. A simple home Bible study or house fellowship is not a church. Compare Titus 1:5. Note that the elders are always mentioned in the plural. There is much freedom within the Bible pattern for the church. One man said, "There is form and there is freedom." The Bible only says that there was a plurality of elders and gives their qualifications. How many there should be and how they share authority and responsibility is determined by each church.

Question areas. I would guess that a house fellowship would not be the same as a church held in a home but the term "house fellowship" leaves a question as to what that is.

Also, it mentions that there are to be elders in a church. What I have found in a couple Independent Baptist Churches in the Columbus, Ohio area, is that there is the Pastor and Deacons but no Elders. That is the way that I think you explained the way it is to be, as the Pastor would be the Elder and Bishop.

Anyway, there seems to be disagreement in that area of Elders in a church, as Cloud's book, if I'm understanding correctly, is saying that there is to be a Pastor and Elders (unless he is using the term Elders to mean Deacons). The church I am now visiting has a pastor and a couple deacons (no Elders) and a deacon teaches Sunday School--which it would seem that Elders would be the ones teaching.

ANSWER #308

As far as Cloud's saying that "*A simple home Bible study or house fellowship is not a church,*" this depends on how this is interpreted. One interpretation would be that he believes there cannot be a "*church*" in a "*home*" or in a "*house.*" If this interpretation is what he means, our 𝕭ible 𝕱or 𝕿oday 𝕭aptist 𝕮hurch is not a "*church*" in his opinion because we meet in our "*house.*" If this is the interpretation, it is definitely unscriptural since there are many references in the New Testament to "*churches*" that met in "*houses.*"

Miscellaneous Questions 71

Here is a study I made on this in 2009. These verses make it crystal clear that there were "*churches*" that met in "*houses.*"

**9 Verses On New Testament House Churches
Either Stated Clearly or Implied
Compiled by Pastor D. A. Waite, Th.D., Ph.D.
January 29, 2009**

Acts 2:46 *And they, continuing daily with one accord in the temple, and **breaking bread from house to house**, did eat their meat with gladness and singleness of heart,*

Acts 20:20 *And how I kept back nothing that was profitable unto you, but have shewed you, and have **taught you publickly, and from house to house**,*

Acts 5:42 *And daily in the temple, and **in every house, they ceased not to teach and preach Jesus Christ**.*

Acts 20:20 *And how I kept back nothing that was profitable unto you, but have shewed you, and have **taught you publickly, and from house to house**,*

Acts 28:30 *And Paul dwelt two whole years **in his own hired house, and received all that came in unto him**,*

Colossians 4:15 *Salute the brethren which are in Laodicea, and Nymphas, and **the church which is in his house**.*

1 Corinthians 16:19 *The churches of Asia salute you. Aquila and Priscilla salute you much in the Lord, with **the church that is in their house**.*

Colossians 4:15 *Salute the brethren which are in Laodicea, and Nymphas, and **the church which is in his house.***

Philemon 2 *And to our beloved Apphia, and Archippus our fellowsoldier, and **to the church in thy house**:*

As far as the "*elders*" question, I interpret the "*elders*" question in the Bible to understand that the churches had multiple pastors-bishops-elders. These are three names for the same office. A lead pastor/bishop/elder can have assistant pastors/bishops/elders as well. They can serve in various capacities, such as (1) for young people's work; (2) for visitation work; (3) for teaching in a Christian school; (4) for teaching in the Sunday School; (5) for leading in the musical ministries of the church, and so on.

I don't believe the Independent Baptist church (Bethel Baptist Church in London, Ontario, Canada) where David Cloud is a member, has a plurality of "*elders*." but I may be wrong. If it does, it is unlike most of the other independent Baptist Churches in our country. The Presbyterians believe in a plurality of elders, but this is not a Baptist distinctive.

> You cannot isolate "*elders*" from also being pastors and bishops. This seems clear from Acts 20:17, (this refers to the "*elders*" of Ephesus); in verse 28 (this says that these "*elders*" are also called by the name of "*overseers*" or "*bishops*"); in verse 28 (this also tells these "*elders*" to "*feed*" or "*pastor*" the "*church of God.*")

This same identification of there being but one office with a combination of these three titles of pastors/bishops/elders is mentioned in 1 Peter chapter 5. 1 Peter 5:1 (Peter addresses the "*elders*"); in verse 2 (these "*elders*" are told to "*feed*" or "*pastor*"); and in verse 2 the "*elders*" are also told to take the "*oversight*" or be a "*bishop*").

1 Timothy 3:1 it is a "*bishop*" in the singular number (although he certainly can have many assistants as needed). In verse 8, the word is "deacons" plural..

> I disagree also that to have a "*church*" you must have a plurality of "*elders*." This would mean that all of the "*house churches*" in the Bible would have had to have "*elders*." I do not think this would have been the case. The Greek word for "*church*" is EKKLESIA. Here are the various meanings of this Greek word:
>
>   1577 ekklesia {ek-klay-see'-ah}
>
>   from a compound of 1537 and a derivative of 2564; TDNT - 3:501,394;
> n f
> AV - church 115, assembly 3; 118
> 1) a gathering of citizens called out from their homes into some
>   public place, an assembly
>   1a) an assembly of the people convened at the public place of the
>   council for the purpose of deliberating
>   1b) the assembly of the Israelites
>   1c) any gathering or throng of men assembled by chance,
>   tumultuously
>   1d) in a Christian sense
>   1d1) **an assembly of Christians** gathered for worship in a
>   religious meeting
>   1d2) a company of Christians, or of those who, hoping for
>   eternal salvation through Jesus Christ, observe their own
>   religious rites, hold their own religious meetings, and
>   manage their own affairs, according to regulations
>   prescribed for the body for order's sake

> 1d3) those who anywhere, in a city, village, constitute such a company and are united into one body
> 1d4) the whole body of Christians scattered throughout the earth
> 1d5) the assembly of faithful Christians already dead and received into heaven

Wise Men And Christmas Gifts

QUESTION #309

Were the wise men wrong in bestowing gifts on Jesus? And if they were not wrong, can I give my kids gifts?

ANSWER #309

You can certainly give gifts to your children any time of the year. Also, remember, the wise men did not come at Jesus birth, the shepherds did. The wise men came when He was a "*young child*" (Matthew 2:8 ff.) of about two years of age.

Calvinism & The Decrees Of God

QUESTION #310

What are the decrees of God?

ANSWER #310

Let me answer this by quoting from a brief paper I have written on "The Decrees of God" as explained in Dr. L. S. Chafer's *Systematic Theology*.

> **The Decrees of God**
> **Written November 9, 2006**
> **By Pastor D. A. Waite, Th.D., Ph.D.**
>
> There are at least four positions on the order of the decrees of God. Only one or two of these agree with the Bible. It should be understood that these are all man-made ideas which have been debated for years by various theologians. This is, for the most part, taken from Dr. L. S. Chafer's Systematic Theology Vol. III, pp. 179 ff. He was my teacher at Dallas Seminary for four years. "LAPSARIAN" means "Fall" and SUPRA, INFRA, and SUB mean "above," "below," and "under," etc. It refers to WHEN "<u>election</u>" took place, either before <u>the fall</u> or after <u>the fall</u>. Here they are:

1. The SUPRALAPSARIAN VIEW (EXTREME LIMITED ATONEMENT) (HYPER-HYPER CALVINISTS)
   a. The decree to <u>elect</u> some to be saved and reprobate all others
   b. The decree to create men both elect and nonelect

c. The decree to permit **the fall**
   d. The decree to provide salvation for the elect
   e. The decree to provide salvation for the elect
2. The INFRALAPSARIAN VIEW   (UNLIMITED ATONEMENT)
   a. The decree to create all men
   b. The decree to permit **the fall.**
   c. The decree to provide salvation for all men
   d. The decree to **elect** those who believe and to leave to just condemnation all who do not believe.
   e. The decree to apply salvation to those who believe.
3. The SUBLAPSARIAN VIEW   (LIMITED ATONEMENT) (HYPER CALVINISTS)
   a. The decree to create all men
   b. The decree to permit **the fall**
   c. The decree to **elect** some and pass over others
   d. The decree to provide salvation for the elect
   e. The decree to apply salvation to the elect
4. The SO-CALLED ARMINIAN VIEW (UNLIMITED ATONEMENT) (FROM THE CALVINIST POINT OF VIEW)
   a. The decree to create all men
   b. The decree to permit **the fall**
   c. The decree to provide salvation to all men
   d. The decree to **elect** on the basis of God's foreknowledge that they would believe
   e. The decree to apply salvation to those who believe.

I believe that both #2 and #4 views are closer to the Bible's position and teaching than either #1 or #3 which I believe to be most unscriptural.

How To Handle Disagreements

QUESTION #311

What should you do when you have a serious disagreement with someone on a Biblical subject?

ANSWER #311

When you are not on the same page with someone, even after discussing the matter carefully, <u>I would just let them alone</u>. Let them follow their own way, but you cannot continue to argue incessantly. You have other ways to spend your time.

Miscellaneous Questions 75

How To Handle Certain Critics

QUESTION #312

Last Saturday, a man from my church who had been into the new versions heard the facts and became a believer in the KJB. He has taken Greek from Nyack College and thought he would run the information by his former professor. His teacher strongly criticized the KJB and the TR underlying it. What do you think?

ANSWER #312

I am sorry this professor tried to discourage your friend. The professor has been fed a group of lies regarding the Greek New Testament. Though Vatican and Sinai were early, they were strongly corrupted by the Gnostic heretics of Alexandria, Egypt. The MSS underlying our KJB are far superior and escaped those corruptions. He has the wrong group of MSS that are corrupt. But this is what he has been taught. I would discourage your friend from talking further with this enemy of the TR and KJB who is teaching a great number of errors.

Making Offerings Public

QUESTION #313

One pastor's congregation raised some suggestion to publicize their offerings openly. They used samples from the Bible that in the Old Testament, offerings from each tribe are published in Numbers chapter 7. In the New Testament, Jesus did teach secret giving.

Matthew 6:3 says: "*But when thou doest alms, let not thy left hand know what thy right hand doeth.*" Are there any teachings from the Bible that can help to decide if the offerings in today's church should be in secret or open?

ANSWER #313

As for making offerings public, I would just say that it is often helpful to the congregation to know the income generally and the outgo generally, in order for them to see how the finances of the church are going generally.

I do not think it is wise or proper to reveal publicly how much various people give to the Lord's work. This must be kept secret and only the treasurer or offering counters should know who gives what, and they should remain silent about what they see when they count the offerings with checks included. Sometimes, sad to say, the treasurer or his assistants talk to others and/or to the pastor, and then sometimes that pastor treats the big givers with partiality and prejudice, which is wrong to do. Also, some pastors, knowing who their large givers are, might bend their messages to suit these people, and never cross them, even if it is in the Words of God.

I think 1 Corinthians 16:1-2 tells us when and how to give and for what good purposes:

1 *"Now concerning the collection for the saints, as I have given order to the churches of Galatia, even so do ye."*

2 *"Upon the first day of the week let every one of you lay by him in store, as God hath prospered him, that there be no gatherings when I come."*

What Does Word-Gender Mean?
QUESTION #314

What is a feminine word? How, why do you designate a word masculine or feminine when identifying a word that is not about gender like *"aunt"* or *"uncle"*? So, what does it mean when you say *"faith"* is feminine in Ephesians 2:8?

ANSWER #314

English does not usually have words that are masculine or feminine. There are a few examples, however, like *"he"* and *"she."* Many other languages, however, like Spanish, French, Latin, Greek, Hebrew, and many others assign gender to all of their nouns. The gender is usually identified in the endings of the words. That means that there are some nouns that are masculine, some that are feminine, and some that are neuter.

How To Order Books From Us
QUESTION #315

I have been trying to work out how to order some books that are on the BFT Website Catalogue. They are:

OP2707 Did Jesus and the Apostles Quote the Septuagint?
     Dr Kirk DiVietro
OP2161 The Septuagint - A Critical Analysis
     Dr Floyd Jones
OP2956 356 Doctrinal Errors in the NIV and Other Modern
     Versions   Dr Jack Moorman
OP1349 Why I reject the New King James Version
     D Cimino

Can you please let me know how to order these?

ANSWER #315

You can order these or any of our materials by going to our website, (www.BibleForToday.org). On the top of the page, you'll see **The BFT Web Store**. Click on that tab and follow the prompts, putting in the BFT numbers one at a time, like 2707, 2161, and 2956 and so on. Then follow the prompts that follow. If you have any more problems in ordering, you can phone us at 856-854-4452.

Divisions In Local Churches

QUESTION #316

It seems we have a young person in the church who is causing division. I will meet with the pastor. This person has started to backbite. What I need is Bible verses to study and bring with me to show this sin in the church. I hope this clears it up some. Thanks for your help.

ANSWER #316

Here are a few verses to go in with you when you meet with the pastor and another person. The verses have to do with speaking evil of things.

Psalm 109:20 "*Let this be the reward of mine adversaries from the LORD, and of them that speak evil against my soul.*"

Titus 3:2 "*To speak evil of no man, to be no brawlers, but gentle, shewing all meekness unto all men.*"

1 Peter 3:16 "*Having a good conscience; that, whereas they speak evil of you, as of evildoers, they may be ashamed that falsely accuse your good conversation in Christ.*"

2 Peter 2:12 "*But these, as natural brute beasts, made to be taken and destroyed, speak evil of the things that they understand not; and shall utterly perish in their own corruption;*"

Jude 1:10 "*But these speak evil of those things which they know not: but what they know naturally, as brute beasts, in those things they corrupt themselves.*"

The following verses show that there must be two or three witnesses to establish every word, rather than relying on hearsay alone.

2 Corinthians 13:1 "*This is the third time I am coming to you. In the mouth of two or three witnesses shall every word be established.*"

1 Timothy 5:19 "*Against an elder receive not an accusation, but before two or three witnesses.*"

The following verses talk about "*busybodies*" and "*tattlers.*"

2 Thessalonians 3:11 "*For we hear that there are some which walk among you disorderly, working not at all, but are busybodies.*"

1 Timothy 5:13 "*And withal they learn to be idle, wandering about from house to house; and not only idle, but tattlers also and busybodies, speaking things which they ought not.*"

I hope these verses are helpful for you in this situation.

Jehovah's Witnesses Material

QUESTION #317

Do you have any tracts I can give the Jehovah's witnesses that come knocking on my door? I had a Jehovah's witness visit me today.

ANSWER #317

Here are the materials we have on the Jehovah's Witnesses: We might not have all of them in stock, but these are the titles. I would strongly advise you to not let any Jehovah's Witnesses into your house. Some of the things they say in their false doctrines might stay with you, your wife, or your children for the rest of their lives and harm you. They will not be convinced. They are trying to convince you. Please follow 2 John 7-11:

> 7 *"For many deceivers are entered into the world, who confess not that Jesus Christ is come in the flesh. This is a deceiver and an antichrist. 8 Look to yourselves, that we lose not those things which we have wrought, but that we receive a full reward. 9 Whosoever transgresseth, and abideth not in the doctrine of Christ, hath not God. He that abideth in the doctrine of Christ, he hath both the Father and the Son. 10 If there come any unto you, and bring not this doctrine, receive him not into your house, neither bid him God speed: 11 For he that biddeth him God speed is partaker of his evil deeds."*

5. The Jehovah's Witnesses Cult

#0272   156 pp. $4.00   Heart To Heart Talks With Jehovah's Witnesses   Duncan, Rev. H

#1309   Cassette $4.00   Hour With Cults--Armstrongism; Mormons; Ch. Sci.; JW's   Waite, Dr. D. A.

#0862   191 pp. $7.00   I Was Raised A Jehovah's Witness   Hewitt, Joe

#2125   110 pp. $11.00   Jehovah's Witnesses And The Person Of Christ   Meadows, Rev. D.

#0381   18 pp. $1.50   On The Wrong Train   Duncan, Rev. H.

#1918   6 pp.   5/$1.50   Reasons (15) Why I Cannot Be A Jehovah's Witness   Mignrd, Robt.

#1569   64 pp. $6.00   Watch Tower, The--A Field White Unto Harvest   Williamson, Pastor John

Miscellaneous Questions

Fasting In This Dispensation
QUESTION :#318
Can you tell me about fasting? and when a Christian should fast? Also what is a true biblical fast?

ANSWER #318
"*Fasting*" is found 17 times in our King James Bible, 9 in the Old Testament and 8 times in the New Testament. It was a custom of the Jews to abstain from food for certain periods of time to give themselves over more completely to worship or service to the Lord uninterrupted by eating. It is not clear that it is an obligation for Christians to observe in this age of Grace, though some do observe it.

Giving And Tithing In The N.T.
QUESTION #319
Last night I heard a sermon at my church about robbing God by not tithing my income according to Malachi chapter3:8. I don't want to be robbing God. I give money whenever I can as much as I can. I do not have a job right now. Will I lose my salvation by not tithing the amount according to Malachi Chapter 3:8?

ANSWER #319
You will not lose your salvation by not tithing your income. This has nothing to do with salvation. Salvation is by God's grace through genuine personal faith in the Lord Jesus Christ as our Saviour apart from any works that we could do or not do.

Giving under the New Testament is "*as God hath prospered*" you. In your case, you are not presently "*prospered*" since you are out of a job, so you can give to the Lord as you are able.

1 Corinthians 16:2 says: "*Upon the first day of the week let every one of you lay by him in store, __as God hath prospered__ him, that there be no gatherings when I come.*"

Are Translations "Inspired" by God?
QUESTION #320
Recently I received this answer to my assertion that "*Translations of God's Hebrew, Aramaic, and Greek Words are not inspired.*" Can you point me to materials or links at Bible for Today or Dean Burgon Society that will answer this brother's assertion? Here is what he wrote:

If a translation can't be inspired . . .

1. All of the conversations that Joseph had "in Egyptian" with Potiphar, and Potiphar's wife, and the Pharaoh's baker, and the Pharaoh's butler, and the Pharaoh himself. All of them are out! because Moses recorded (translated) them into Hebrew when he wrote Genesis.
2. Out go all the conversations that Moses had with the Pharaoh of Egypt in his language.
3. Out go the renderings of the conversations Abraham had with the king and people of Sodom when he rescued them.
4 Out go the conversations that David had with one of the kings among the Philistines.
5. Out go the conversations Naomi had with Ruth, (salvable only by insisting that it had to be Hebrew).
6. Out go the renderings in the original of what was on Jesus' cross in Latin, Greek, and Hebrew.
7. Out go Jesus' exchange with Pilate.
8. Out go Paul's testimonies to Festus.
9. Out go all the Greek-language renderings in the original autographs of Matthew and Luke of the genealogies, since their original language was actually Hebrew.
10. Out go the quotes of the words spoken between Nehemiah and Sanballat.
11. Out go the translations of what was spoken between Nehemiah and Artaxerxes.
12. Out go the translations of the conversations between Esther and King Ahasuerus, and the quotes from Vashti his first queen, and Haman's commandments to his servants and his own conferences with the king.
13. Out go all the quotes included in the story of Balaam and the pagan elders of Moab and Midian in Numbers 22.

ANSWER #320

All 13 of these so-called "*translations*" are ridiculous examples of whether or not "*translations*" can be "*inspired of God,*" "*inspired,*" or "*God-breathed.*" We're not talking about "*translating of phrases in the Bible*" all of which were given by inspiration of God. We're talking about "*translations*" from the Hebrew, Aramaic, and Greek Words underlying the King James Bible into various languages of the world.

None of the various Bible "*translations*" in any language whatever can be called "*given by inspiration of God,*" "*inspired of God,*" "*inspired,*" or "*God-breathed.*" Only the Hebrew, Aramaic, and Greek Words of the Bible qualify for any of these terms. Otherwise, you have very serious Peter Ruckman and Gail Riplinger heresies.

If Bad, Why Is "Negro" Still Used?
QUESTION #321
I must admit that I was a bit saddened to hear your use of the word *"Negro"* to describe black people. *"Negro,"* as you well know is an offensive term, and regardless of how it is used, it is always perceived in the negative. I am sure you mean no offense when you use the term–but it truly is offensive.
ANSWER #321
As far as "*Negro*" is concerned, this is the Spanish, French, Italian, and Latin for "*black*" and is a perfectly good word. I am sorry that some think it is a smear term. "*Nigger*" certainly would be a smear word, but not "*Negro*." I looked up reputable current organizations that use this word in a respectful manner as I do. Here is a list:

United **Negro** College Fund

Negro Leagues Baseball Museum

Negro Spirituals and **Negro** Spirituals.com

National Council of **Negro** Women

The Journal of **Negro** History

The Journal of **Negro** Education

The Universal **Negro** Improvement Association

Negro Periodicals in the United States

If the English word, *"Negro,"* is really *"offensive,"* why is it used in these eight groups, and perhaps many others? Why not write to all eight of these organizations and ask them to change their name, eliminating the word, *"Negro,"* because it is *"offensive"* to some people. Let me know what they say. In the light of that, I might rethink or confirm my own use of the word. As it now stands, I believe linguistically, it is a perfectly good term. Those who believe it is not be used perhaps should not listen to the groups who are against its use.

Burgon's Position On The T.R.
QUESTION #322
From the following quotes, it seemed that Burgon believed that the Traditional or Received Text was in need of revision. To me, this seems contradictory to what most men in the Dean Burgon Society believe. They seem to believe in the perfection of the Received Text and that it has been perfectly preserved. If this is true, obviously, it would not need revision. It seems obvious, from the quotes below, that Burgon did not believe this. Is there a real contradiction here or am I misunderstanding something?

ANSWER #322

You are correct that Dean Burgon believed that the Textus Receptus needed some revision in minor details. He also said that it was good as it then stood and would never lead anyone seriously astray who used it. Here is the full quotation from Dean Burgon. It is found on page 269 of Dean Burgon's *Revision Revised* (BFT #611 @ $25.00 + $5.00 S&H). Dean Burgon wrote:

"Beyond all question the Textus Receptus is the dominant Graeco-Syrian Text of A.D. 359 to A.D. 400. Obtained from a variety of sources, this Text proves to be essentially the same in all. **That it requires Revision in respect of many of its lesser details, is undeniable**: but it is at least as certain that it is an excellent Text as it stands, and that **the use of it will never lead critical students of Scripture seriously astray**,–which is what no one will venture to predicate concerning any single Critical Edition of the N.T. which has been published since the days of Griesbach, by the disciples of Griesbach's school."

We of the Dean Burgon Society (of which I have been the President since its beginning over 32 years ago) know about Dean Burgon's assessment and never deny his position on it. However, he said the time for such minor "*revision*" had not yet come in his day. In my book, *Burgon's Warnings on Revision* (BFT #804 @ $8.00 + $4.00 S&H) I quote from Dean Burgon's *Revision Revised* showing at least a minimum of 14 requirements that must be present before such a revision of these lesser details. Because these 14 requirements are not present and probably will never be present, our DBS has not sought to revise the Greek Words underlying our KJB. We accept them as they now are and believe them to have been preserved as promised in the Bible.

The ACCC And The Bible Issues

QUESTION #323

I just heard a taped recording of the American Council of Christian Churches (ACCC) panel discussion on Contemporary Evangelicalism and it does seem to me that they are somewhat disoriented on what to do with the declining fundamentalism among younger men in their ranks today who choose to be trained in neo-evangelical schools.

What is sad is that the panelists conveniently brushed away the whole issue of Bible versions and did not answer a couple of legitimate questions that were asked in regard to this battle for the Bible. The panel was comprised of Dr Ralph Colas, Dr Richard Harris, and Dr Rolland McCune.

Miscellaneous Questions 83

ANSWER #323
I looked at the LINK from McCune and noticed an ad for the English Standard Version (ESV). This tells where he is heading. He is a firm believer in the Critical Text. Though Colas and Harris may use the KJB, they have caved in to the pressure of Bob Jones University on textual matters and want to continue to be friendly with those who support the Gnostic Critical Greek Text, who deny Bible Preservation of the Hebrew, Aramaic, and Greek Words, and who undermine our KJB by so doing.

I used to be a strong part of the ACCC in years gone by. I was Chairman of the Radio and Audio Film Commission at one time. As you might remember, there was a battle with Dr. McIntire when he attempted to "*takeover*" the ACCC during an intermission in the meetings, with which takeover I did not agree. I left the employ of the ACCC and began our Bible For Today ministry since it was difficult for them financially and also it was difficult for me to have 5 or 6 bosses dictating what I should write and say. Since then, I have noticed a strong BJU influence of speakers and programs.

Errors of Baptist "Bride" & "Body"
QUESTION #324
We have met a strange doctrine over here and was wondering what you knew of it. It is called the "*Baptist Bride*." What do you know of it?

ANSWER #324
http://www.deceptioninthechurch.com/baptist_bride.htm gives a critical review of this Baptist Bride teaching.
http://www.baptistpillar.com/bd0341.htm is an article which favors this Baptist Bride teaching.
http://www.baptistpillar.com/bd0118.htm is another article favoring Baptist Bride and even Baptist "Body."
http://www.baptistsonline.org/baptist_bride.htm is an entire book favoring the Baptist Bride position.
http://www.blessedquietness.com/journal/housechu/bapbride.htm is another critical article on the Baptist Bride position.

I do not agree with the "Baptist Bride" or the "Baptist Body" position. It means that only certain clearly defined Baptist churches (and faithful people in them) all over the world are members of the "*bride*" of Christ and none other. All other saved people who are not members of these special churches, though going to Heaven, are in an inferior status. They are only called by this group the "*friends of the bridegroom*," but are not considered by them to be members of Christ's "*bride*." Though these people seem to be otherwise good Christian

> people, I do not find this position supported by Scripture and therefore I believe it to be unscriptural and therefore false. I believe that every born-again, redeemed, saved Christian is a member of both the "*bride*" of Christ and the "*body*" of Christ. To limit these terms to a certain kind of "Baptists" is heretical and unscriptural.

How Far Should Separation Go?
QUESTION #325

On the teaching tape in 2 Corinthians 6:14 and on the part of being separate from unbelievers, it is mentioned that we are not to be "*unequally yoked together with unbelievers.*" The examples are given of marriage, business partners, and close friendships. Also, it was mentioned that we can still associate with others such as personnel at the store, fireman, policeman who are unbelievers. What about the situation where there would be Christian firemen working with unbelieving firemen? They are yoked together in staying in firemen quarters, working together in fighting fires--in a way like business partners. It seems difficult to me to separate this whole thing out. During apostolic times, it is difficult to imagine Paul sending someone from one of his churches to someone outside the church who would be a heathen for medical advice.

> ### ANSWER #325
> I do not believe we should "*associate*" with unbelievers in a close, intimate, personal way. But in a business sense of going into a gas station and buying gas, a Christian should not be afraid to have an unsaved station attendant pump his gas.
>
> When going into a drug store to buy a pen, it is not incumbent on a Christian to insist that the clerk is a Christian. It is close association and close fellowship that Christians must avoid. The following verses pertain to this subject of Biblical separation.

Ephesians 5:11 "*And have no fellowship with the unfruitful works of darkness, but rather reprove them.*"

1 Corinthians 5:9 "*I wrote unto you in an epistle not to company with fornicators*:
10 *Yet not altogether with the fornicators of this world, or with the covetous, or extortioners, or with idolaters; for then must ye needs go out of the world. . . .*"

The Lord Jesus Christ prayed to God the Father as follows in John 17:15: "*I pray not that thou shouldest take them out of the world, but that thou shouldest keep them from the evil.*"

Separation And Prayer Requests

QUESTION #326

I have a question in an area of Scriptural separation. How far does one go in separating? Can we pray for prayer requests for our country's safety if we would not agree with the Biblical positions of those on the committee for such a group? This is where I struggle with separatism. Is there something of an intersection of doctrine and God's grace involved in all of this?

ANSWER #326

If these people are saved, we can certainly love them in the Lord, but we cannot follow their unbiblical practices. As for their "prayer requests," they might be fine (as you say they are), so long as they are Biblical and proper. But be sure that, in praying for these requests, you do not take away the time needed for praying for requests that Bible-believing and separated Christians have which are never mentioned by these other groups. Their requests might be good, but genuine needs of faithful, obedient Christians are much better and best.

"Whosoever" Vs. "Whoever"

QUESTION #327

What is the difference between "*whosoever*" and "*whoever*"? The KJB exclusively translates using "*whosoever*," while the versions use "*whoever*." Is the correct Greek PAS or PASA? What is the difference between the translation of "*every one*" (PAS) as in Mark 9:49 and "*whosoever*" (PAS) in John 3:16?

ANSWER #327

One dictionary gave "*whosoever*" as an emphatic form of "*whoever*." They generally mean the same thing. Other forms of this are "*whomsoever*" and "*whosesoever*" depending on the sentence structure.

PAS is masculine and goes with masculine nouns. PASA is feminine and goes with feminine nouns. It is the same Greek word and means the same thing.

I think that PAS translated as either "*every one*" or "*each*" or "*whoever*" or "*whosoever*" is all right. It depends on the context as to which translation might suit the best. In Mark 9:49, PAS is individual and "*every one*" or "*each one*" would fit. "*Whosoever*" or "*whoever*" is general and would not fit as well. The same is true in Mark 9:49 of the PASA for "*every sacrifice*." "*Each*" or "*every*" would fit here because it is individual. "*Whosoever*" or "*whoever*" (general) would not fit. The context determines it.

Leading In Prayer With Unsaved
QUESTION #328
This past Saturday my mom asked me to lead in prayer for an early Thanksgiving family lunch. Several of the people there were not Christians. Did I make a mistake in by leading in prayer for the lunch? What is your advice the next time a similar situation comes around again?
ANSWER #328
If your Mom asked you to lead in prayer to thank the Lord for the food, I think this is all right, even though those at the meal were not all saved. You are thanking the Lord, not other people.

NIV's 356 Doctrinal Passage Errors
QUESTION #329
Please tell me do you have the book "*THREE HUNDRED FIFTY-SIX DOCTRINAL ERRORS IN THE NIV AND OTHER MODERN BIBLE VERSIONS*" by Jack Moorman.
ANSWER #329
We have this book as **BFT #2956 @ $10.00 + $6.00 S&H**. This is in copy machine format. In Dr. Moorman's book, *Early Manuscripts, :Church Fathers and the Authorized Version* (**BFT #3230 # $20.00 + $8.00 S&H**) he has listed these 356 passages in almost 200 pages. This is a printed book. You can order either of these for this information.

The Omnipresence of Jesus Christ
QUESTION #330
In the King James Bible, John 3:13 reads: "*And no man hath ascended up to heaven, but he that came down from heaven, even the Son of man* **which is in heaven**." The Critical Greek Text omits "*which is in heaven.*" How does this influence the doctrine of Christ?
ANSWER #330
I have used this verse many times to prove the Lord Jesus Christ's omnipresence. It has sound documentation for being included in the King James Bible's New Testament as it stands. The Gnostic Critical Greek Text which omits "*which is in heaven*" is in error. The Greek word which is translated "*is*" in this verse is a present participle. This indicates that, as to the Lord Jesus Christ's deity, He is now, was then, and will be continuously "*in heaven*" as well as everywhere else. As to His deity, He was, is, and ever will be omnipresent.

Degrees Of Punishment In Hell
QUESTION #331
I wondered if there is an explanation available explaining the different degrees of punishment in Hell.

ANSWER #331
I believe the Bible is clear that there are degrees of punishment in Hell, just as I believe it is clear that there are degrees of blessings in Heaven, some receiving rewards and some receiving no rewards.

Here are some of the verses showing that there are degrees of punishment in Hell. The key words are *"more tolerable"* and *"in the day of judgment."*

Matthew 10:14-15

*"And whosoever shall not receive you, nor hear your words, when ye depart out of that house or city, shake off the dust of your feet. Verily I say unto you, It shall be **more tolerable** for the land of Sodom and Gomorrha **in the day of judgment**, than for that city."*

Matthew 11:23-24

*"And thou, Capernaum, which art exalted unto heaven, shalt be brought down to hell: for if the mighty works, which have been done in thee, had been done in Sodom, it would have remained until this day. But I say unto you, That it shall be **more tolerable** for the land of Sodom **in the day of judgment**, than for thee."*

Mark 6:11

*"And whosoever shall not receive you, nor hear you, when ye depart thence, shake off the dust under your feet for a testimony against them. Verily I say unto you, It shall be **more tolerable** for Sodom and Gomorrha **in the day of judgment**, than for that city."*

Luke 10:10-15

*"But into whatsoever city ye enter, and they receive you not, go your ways out into the streets of the same, and say, Even the very dust of your city, which cleaveth on us, we do wipe off against you: notwithstanding be ye sure of this, that the kingdom of God is come nigh unto you. But I say unto you, that it shall be **more tolerable in that day** for Sodom, than for that city. Woe unto thee, Chorazin! woe unto thee, Bethsaida! for if the mighty works had been done in Tyre and Sidon, which have been done in you, they had a great while ago repented, sitting in sackcloth and ashes. But it shall be **more tolerable** for Tyre and Sidon **at the judgment**, than for you. And thou, Capernaum, which art exalted to heaven, shalt be thrust down to hell."*

This is the basis of degrees of punishment in Hell. All unsaved will go there, but the more light that has been rejected the less "*tolerable*" will be the punishment "*in the day of judgment*."

The Rapture Is Imminent

QUESTION #332

If I am correct, when the "*times of the gentiles*" (Luke 21:24) is fulfilled, that is when we believe the rapture will take place, is it not?

ANSWER #332

I do not believe there is any prophecy that must be fulfilled before the rapture of the believers. It is imminent, that is, it may occur at any time without having to be preceded by any prophetic event. There are some things to be fulfilled, however, before the Lord's second phase of His coming to earth to set up his millennial reign.

Ruckman/Riplinger KJB Heresies

QUESTION #333

I was listening to one of your audio sermons a few days ago and noticed that you do not agree with Dr. Peter Ruckman and his position in the King James Only debate. For this, I commend you. I noticed, however, that in the end of *The Revision Revised*, you make mention of Mrs. Riplinger and her book *New Age Bible Versions*. I have a copy of this book and gave up on reading it because of its frequent use of quotes taken out of context and ideas of a grand conspiracy theory. I believe her method and conclusions are very wrong. Do you agree with Mrs. Riplinger, even though she frequently exhibits poor scholarship in her research and writing?

ANSWER #333

We used to carry *NEW AGE BIBLE VERSIONS*, though I did not agree in some of her conclusions. We have since dropped that book and carry none of Gail Riplinger's books. In fact, I have recently written a book entitled *A WARNING!! On Gail Riplinger's KJB & Multiple Inspiration HERESY* (**BFT #3464 @ $13.00 + $7.00 S&H**). There is much evidence substantiating your "*quotes out of context*" errors you have discovered. It is available free as a PDF document upon E-mail request from anyone around the world.

The Beginning Of The Church

QUESTION #334
When did the church begin? Why is there a Baptist church.

ANSWER #334
I believe the Lord Jesus Christ is the Foundation of the *"church which is His Body"* composed of every born-again Christian from the Day of Pentecost until the rapture.

*"And hath put all things under his feet, and gave him to be the head over all things to **the church, which is his body**, the fulness of him that filleth all in all."* (Ephesians 1:22-23)

The church was predicted to be established in the future by the Lord Jesus Christ.

*"And I say also unto thee, That thou art Peter, and upon this rock **I will build my church**; and the gates of hell shall not prevail against it."* (Matthew 16:18)

The *"church which is His body"* began and was empowered by God the Holy Spirit on the Day of Pentecost (Acts 2) Whom the Lord Jesus Christ, its resurrected Head, had sent to earth from Heaven as He promised.

Our church is a Bible-believing Baptist church because we believe that Baptist doctrines and practices come the closest to any other group to the doctrines and practices found in the New Testament.

Lesbianism & Homosexuality

QUESTION #335
I saw your email on a Christian site that also mentioned things on homosexuality. I wonder if you consider same sex romantic love a sin? Where is lesbianism condemned as a sin in the Old Testament? Where does Jesus condemn same sex love and homosexuality? Why is there no law in the main 10 commandments from God to condemn gay people and why is the whole Bible silent on same sex romantic love if it's a sin? And why did the early church sanction same sex unions if it is also a sin? With so much silence, how is the Bible so clear it is a sin?

ANSWER #335
The Bible is crystal clear that homosexuality or lesbianism or same sex *"romantic love"* is an abomination and gross sin. These sins were one of the basic reasons why God destroyed the cities of Sodom and Gomorrah. I have listed below a number of verses against homosexuality of all kinds.

Let me ask you a few questions that arise out of your questions. Are you a homosexual yourself, either male or female? Do you really want to know where the Bible condemns homosexuality and lesbianism, or do you just want to argue. If you are a homosexual, do you want to repent of it and to change your lifestyle, or just remain as you are? Where do you live? What state are you in? Where did you get my "e-mail" that you mentioned? On what website? I have no more time to write about this, but if you will call me at **856-854-4747**, I will be glad to talk with you about it.

The following are some of the Scriptures that condemn homosexuality and bestiality, whether by males or females.

The Bible Against Homosexuality and Bestiality
From Pastor D. A. Waite, Th.D., Ph.D.

Leviticus 18:22

22 *Thou shalt not lie with mankind, as with womankind: it is abomination.* (KJV) [MALE HOMOSEXUALITY]

Leviticus 18:23

23 *Neither shalt thou lie with any beast to defile thyself therewith: neither shall any woman stand before a beast to lie down thereto: it is confusion.* [MALE OR FEMALE BESTIALITY]

Leviticus 20:13

13 *If a man also lie with mankind, as he lieth with a woman, both of them have committed an abomination: they shall surely be put to death; their blood shall be upon them.* (KJV) [MALE HOMOSEXUALITY]

1 Corinthians 6:9

9 *Know ye not that the unrighteous shall not inherit the kingdom of God? Be not deceived: neither fornicators, nor idolaters, nor adulterers, nor effeminate, nor abusers of themselves with mankind,* (KJV) [MALE HOMOSEXUALITY]

1 Timothy 1:10

10 *For whoremongers, for them that defile themselves with mankind, for menstealers, for liars, for perjured persons, and if there be any other thing that is contrary to sound doctrine;* (KJV) [MALE HOMOSEXUALITY]

Romans 1:27

27 *And likewise also the men, leaving the natural use of the woman, burned in their lust one toward another; men with men working that which is unseemly, and receiving in themselves that recompence of their error which was meet.* (KJV) [MALE HOMOSEXUALITY]

Romans 1:26

26 *For this cause God gave them up unto vile affections: for even their*

Miscellaneous Questions

women did change the natural use into that which is against nature: (KJV) [FEMALE HOMOSEXUALITY OR LESBIANISM]
Genesis 19:5
   5 *And they called unto Lot, and said unto him, Where are the men which came in to thee this night? bring them out unto us, that we may know them.* (KJV) [MEN OF SODOM--MALE HOMOSEXUALS]
Judges 19:22
   22 *Now as they were making their hearts merry, behold, the men of the city, certain sons of Belial, beset the house round about, and beat at the door, and spake to the master of the house, the old man, saying, Bring forth the man that came into thine house, that we may know him.* (KJV) [MALE HOMOSEXUALS]

Assurance Of Salvation

QUESTION #336

I came out of a very strong charismatic/Pentecostal background. However, along the way, I got sidetracked by a friend who was a strong Calvinist. I started to read and listen to Calvinistic teachings and got very involved with Calvinism. I always knew inside of me that something did not sit right with Calvinism. Anyway the long and the short of it is this, the effects of being exposed to Calvinistic teaching has left me with a very big struggle with assurance of salvation. What concerns me is why do I struggle so much with assurance? I would appreciate our counsel on this.

ANSWER #336

Assurance of salvation, as salvation itself, is a matter of genuine heart-felt faith in God's Words. The same Words that assure us of eternal life by genuine personal faith in the Lord Jesus Christ are the Words that assure us that this salvation is secure and assured. You must trust God's Words for your assurance. If you can't trust God's Words for your eternal salvation, you can't trust His Words for your eternal assurance. On the contrary, if you can trust God's Words for your eternal salvation, you can trust His Words for your eternal assurance.

Salvation For The Pope & Catholics

QUESTION #337

Q1: Can the Pope of Rome be saved? Why or why not?

Q2: Can the Roman Catholics be saved and still stay in the Roman Catholic Church? Why or why not?

ANSWER #337

Q1 It is highly unlikely if the pope believes **all** of the doctrines of the Roman Catholic church. However, "*With men this is impossible; but with God all things are possible.*" (Matthew 19:26)

Q2 It is highly unlikely if these Roman Catholics believe **all** of the doctrines of the Roman Catholic Church. However, "*With men this is impossible; but with God all things are possible.*" (Matthew 19:26)

Erasmus And The KJB

QUESTION #338

I'm a believer and have a "*Defined King James Bible*" that I study on a daily basis. One of my friends claims that Erasmus was a Catholic and therefore the King James Version is similar to the Catholic versions. Was he a Catholic?

ANSWER #338

Yes, Erasmus was a Roman Catholic, but not in the good graces of the Pope. He refused a Cardinal's hat. His books were banned by the Pope. His New Testament was printed both in Latin and in Greek rather than in Latin alone. He was buried in a Protestant cemetery. I have seen a picture of his grave in that cemetery. Aside from this twisted belief, the King James Bible was not based on Erasmus' edition of 1516, but on Beza's 5th edition, 1598, 82 years after Erasmus.

Here are some of the materials we have on Erasmus:

BFT #2609 11 pages $1.50 Erasmus--A Minuscule Biography By Pastor Bob Steward

BFT #2490 Cassette $4.00 Erasmus/T.R. & Computers & Testimonies By Dave Hollowood and Dr. Kirk DiVietro

BFT #2656 27 pages $3.00 In Defense of Erasmus--16 Questions & Answers About Erasmus by Dr. John Cereghin

BFT #2448 34 pages $3.50 Myths About the King James Bible--Myth 1 Erasmus a Humanist By David Cloud

BFT #2456 12 pages $1.50 That Rascal Erasmus--Defense of his Greek Text By Daryl Coats

The RVG & Spanish Bible Issues
QUESTION #339
I'm behind the RVG, and it frustrated me to come across the article and the chart that was included in the previous email. The war over the Spanish Bible was what led me to read/study your book on Defending the KJB (and start studying Greek) because there are those that are slighting the origins of the KJB in minor ways that really challenged me to study up and find the truth of the KJB and it's origins. Where did this chart come from?

ANSWER #339
I do not know who made up this chart to damage the RVG by giving false information. I'll send a copy of this to Dr. Humberto Gomez, the editor of the RVG, so he can be aware of this false information that is being circulated against his work.

The RVG & Spanish Bible Issues
QUESTION #340
I recently came across the chart below. I know that you cover the textual variations of the different TR in your book and wondered if you could briefly inform me again of the which one the KJV was translated from. I know that it is not the Stephanus 1550 because I checked and the word "Gospel/evangelio" was not in it. If you have some info you can send me on the variations of the TR that would be very helpful. Thanks!

Reference
Word omitted
Reina-Valera 1960
Textus Receptus
Stephanus 1550
RVG
Acts 8:12
evangelio
omitted
Acts 10:36
evangelio
omitted
Acts 15:35
evangelio
omitted
Acts 17:18

evangelio
omitted

ANSWER #340

The KJB was translated from Beza's 5th edition, 1598.

You are not correct that "gospel/evengelio" is omitted in the RVG or in the KJB. The word, *"gospel"* is used 35 times in the King James Bible. I would expect it is used also 35 times in the RVG Spanish.

The word used in this list is not EUANGELION (noun for "*gospel*") but EUANGELIZO (verb for either "*preach the gospel*" or just "*preach*" which it is so translated 23 times in the KJB. In Acts 15:35 for instance, it would not make sense to translate it "*preach the gospel the word of the Lord.*" The same strange sense is true in 8:12, "*preaching the gospel the kingdom of God*" and Acts 10:36 "*preaching the gospel peace.*" And in Acts 17:18 "*preached the gospel unto them Jesus.*" I hope you understand what I am saying here.

The RVG & Spanish Bible Issues
QUESTION #341

I found out there is a Spanish Bible called Reina Valera version 1960. Once in a while I visit the web site of Middletown Bible Church and mentioned to Pastor Zeller about the Spanish Bible and Brother Gomez. Pastor Zeller mentioned that they use the Spanish Bible called Reina Valera Version 1960. Is that version based on the TR? Also, what is the name of the Bible that Brother Gomez worked on? Pastor George said they had found the Reina Valera Version 1960 reliable. Is there an example of a translation problem that you could send me concerning the Reina Valera Version 1960?

ANSWER #341

Pastor Zeller is friendly toward me and we have written e-mails back and forth. We agree on separation and many Biblical things, but we part company on the KJB and the TR underlying it. He was trained, as I was, in the Critical Greek Text (CT), and so is comfortable with the Reina Valera 1960 which is loaded with Critical Textual variations. I wouldn't trouble him about these because if he thinks the CT is better than the Textus Receptus (TR), he wouldn't see any reason to change.

Dr. Humberto Gomez began with the 1909 Spanish which is better than the 1960, but still had many errors. These he corrected. His Bible (which we carry) is called the RVG (Reina Valera Gomez). It is true to the TR in the New Testament.

I don't have a 1960 handy, but if you have one, check out the following verses. You might possibly find CT readings in such verses as:

1. Romans 1:16 (no por Christo)

2. Philippians 4:13 (no por Christo)
3. John 5:47 (no por mi)
4. 1 Timothy 3:16 (no "God manifested in the flesh" no dios)
5. John 5:7-8 (part of 7 and part of 8 missing)

And probably 356 places in all as mentioned by Dr. Jack Moorman in his book. As I said, I wouldn't waste your time developing these with Pastor Zeller (unless of course he asks for them).
http://www.biblefortoday.org/idx_foreign_bible_versions.htm has some information on the Spanish 1960 edition that you can study also.

John MacArthur & Christ's Blood

QUESTION #342

John MacArthur is a man of sound Biblical doctrine. I have examined his position on the blood very carefully. He has tried and tried to clear this issue up. Read the article, "*I Believe In The Precious Blood*" by John MacArthur. I understand completely that the blood had to be applied. I believe that MacArthur understands that as well. He simply does not want the blood to become mysticism. It is the belief in Christ that applies the blood. If this were not the case, then the blood splattering on non-believing Roman Soldiers would have saved them. We are saved by Grace through faith. Without the blood shed, the death and the resurrection, there would be no redemption of sin. John understands this. He really does. If he denied the vicarious blood atonement, I would also be finished with him! But he doesn't.

ANSWER #342

You are dead wrong on John MacArthur's position on the Blood of Christ. If you read the article mentioned ("*I Believe In The Precious Blood*"), very, very, very carefully, you will discover that he still defines the Bible word, "*blood*" as only a figure of speech or metonym for "*death*" in some way. This is a heresy for him to redefine "*blood*" as "*death*." When the Bible speaks of fourteen things accomplished by the "blood" of the Lord Jesus Christ, it means these things were literally accomplished by the "*blood*," and not alone by His "*death*." John MacArthur still clings to his heresy on the Blood of Christ!, despite his article with the confusing title, "*I Believe In The Precious Blood*." I recommend you read my book on *John MacArthur's Heresy On The Blood of Christ* (**BFT #2185 @ $5.00 + $3.00 S&H**).

As you can see from the titles listed below, there are many others who hold my view on this and reject the questioner's view.

Here are some other articles we have available exposing MacArthur's heresy on the Blood of Christ.
BFT #1426, 4 pp., 3/$1.50 , Another Look At MacArthur And The Blood Of

Christ, Bynum, Pastor E. L.
BFT #1740/1-3, ("C" refers to Cassette) Cassettes, $15.00, Blood Of Christ Defined/Defended Against MacArthur, Waite, Dr. D. A.
BFT #1740/VCR, $15.00, Blood Of Christ Defined/Defended Against MacArthur, Waite, Dr. D. A.
BFT #1595/3, C, $4.00, Blood Of Christ, The, And John MacArthur's Heresy, Waite, Dr. D. A.
BFT #1525TP ("TP" refers to tape), C, $4.00, Blood Of Christ, The--Is MacArthur A Heretic On It?, Waite, Dr. D. A.
BFT #1525VCR, $15.00, Blood Of Christ, The--Is MacArthur A Heretic On It?, Waite, Dr. D. A.
BFT #1524, C, $4.00, Blood Of Christ, The--John MacArthur's Error, Waite, Dr. D. A.
BFT #1744/1-3, C, $9.00, Blood Of Christ, The--MacArthur Answered In Liberia, Waite, Dr. D. A.
BFT #1451-P, 38 pp., $4.00, Blood Of Christ, The--MacArthur's Heresy, 3 Sermons, Waite, Dr. D. A.
BFT #1451/1-2, C, $7.00, Blood Of Christ, The--MacArthur's Heresy, 3 Sermons, Waite, Dr. D. A.
BFT #1451VCR, $15.00, Blood Of Christ, The--MacArthur's Heresy, 3 Sermons, Waite, Dr. D. A.
BFT #1401TP, C, $4.00, Blood Of Christ, The--John MacArthur's Heresy On It, Waite, Dr. D. A.
BFT #1401VCR, $15.00, Blood Of Christ, The--John MacArthur's Heresy On It, Waite, Dr. D. A.
BFT #1471, C, $4.00, Blood Of Christ--Answer To Dr. John MacArthur, Rasmussen, Dr. Roland
BFT #1744VC2, $15.00, Blood Of Christ--Bible Vs. MacArthur (#2) (Liberia), Waite, Dr. D. A.
BFT #1663, C, $4.00, Blood Of Sprinkling, The--John MacArthur's Heresy, Jones, Dr. Bob, Jr.,
BFT #2028, C, $4.00, Defending Christ's Blood--How MacArthur Is Wrong, Streeter, Pastor Lloyd L.
BFT #1721, 3 pp., 2/$1.50, Denying The Literal Blood Of Christ--Exposing Wrong, Paisley, Dr. Ian R. K.
BFT #2295, 34 pp., $3.50, Detroit Baptist Theological Sem.--Heresy On Christ's Blood!, Streeter, Pastor Lloyd L.
BFT #1473, C, $4.00, Fake Preachers--Exposing Swaggert, Baaker, & MacArthur, Lacy, Dr. Al.,
BFT #1666, 10 pp., $3.00, God's Miracle Blood--Refutation Of John MacArthur, Beebe, Dr. Walter

Miscellaneous Questions

BFT #1556, C, $4.00, Heresy Of John MacArthur On Blood Of Christ, The, Gray, Dr. Bob,

BFT #1415, 3 pp., 2/$1.50, John MacArthur And The Blood Of Christ, Bynum, Pastor E. L.

BFT #1420, 2 pp., 2/$1.50, John MacArthur Minimizes The Blood Of Christ, Malone, Dr. Tom,

BFT #1470, C, $4.00, John MacArthur On The Blood & Other Errors, Gray, Dr. Bob

BFT #1528-P, 3pp., 2/$1.50, John MacArthur Refuses To Recant Error On The Blood, Rasmussen, Dr. Roland

BFT #1565, 6pp., 2/$2.00, John MacArthur Refuses To Recant On Christ's Blood, Rasmussen, Dr. Roland

BFT #1620, 10pp. $2.00, John MacArthur's 'Quadruple' By-Pass Of The Truth, Stanford, Miles .J.,

BFT #1589, 6pp., 2/$2.00, John MacArthur's Errors On The Blood Of Christ, Edwin, Rev.W.

BFT #2185, 65pp, $6.00 John MacArthur's Heresy On Christ's Blood --Printed Booklet, Waite, Dr. D. A.

BFT #1638, C, $4.00, John MacArthur's Heresy On The Blood Of Christ, Waite, Dr. D. A.

BFT #1400, 134, $14.00, John MacArthur's Heresy On The Blood Of Christ-- 1st Edition, Waite, Dr. D. A.

BFT #2746, 9pp., $2.00, John MacArthur's Heresy on the Blood--important Answer, Dickerson, Dr. Allen P.

BFT #1930VCR, $15.00, John MacArthur's Heresy Refuted + Ruckman's Errors, Waite, Dr. D. A.

BFT #1930TP, C, $4.00, John MacArthur's Heresy Refuted By His Own Voice, Waite, Dr. D. A.

BFT #1719-TP, C, $4.00, John MacArthur--Condemned By His Own Voice! (C.P.),Waite, Dr. D. A.

BFT #1719VCR, $15.00, John MacArthur--Condemned By His Own Voice! (C.P.),Waite, Dr. D. A.

BFT #1715-TP, C, $4.00, John MacArthur--Condemned By His Own Voice! (L.A.),Waite, Dr. D. A.

BFT #1715-VCR, $15.00, John MacArthur--Condemned By His Own Voice! (L.A.),Waite, Dr. D. A.

BFT #1870, 2pp., 2/$2.00, John MacArthur--Dropped By 3 Stations For Heresy, Editorial

BFT #2184, 8pp. ,2/$2.00, John MacArthur--What Is His Theology? (Three Areas), Woodbridge, Dr. Charles

BFT #2552, 13pp. $3.00, MacArthur Heresy Invades Fund. Baptists--IBFNA,

Waite, Dr. D. A.
BFT #1466, 3pp., 2/$2.00, MacArthur's Dangerous Views On The Blood, Nickerson, E.
BFT #1968/1, C, $4.00, MacArthur's Heresies On "Lordship" & Christ's Blood, Waite, Dr. D. A.
BFT #2017, C, $4.00, MacArthur's Heresies On The Blood Refuted On Radio, Waite, Dr. D. A.
BFT #1992, 5pp., 2/$2.00, MacArthur's Heresy On Christ's Blood--27 Problems, Murphy, Mrs. B.
BFT #1710-P, 15pp., $3.00, MacArthur's Selected Quotes On Christ's Blood (49 Selections), Waite, Dr. D. A.
BFT #1710-TP, C, $4.00, MacArthur's Voice On The Blood (49 Selections), Waite, Dr. D. A.
BFT #1580, 11 pp., $2.00, Pastoral Letter On MacArthur's Heresy On The Blood, Rasmussen, Dr. Roland
BFT #1884, C, $4.00, Precious Blood Of Christ, The--Answering MacArthur, Pietryle, Dr.A,
BFT #1574, 7pp., 2/$2.00, Precious Blood Of Christ, The--MacArthur's Heresy, Steward, Rev. Bob
BFT #1697, C, $4.00, Swindoll's Ministry Now Follows MacArthur On Christ's Blood, Hymers, Dr. R. L.
BFT #2799VCR, $15.00, The Blood of Christ--Refuting MacArthur, Defending the Truth, Waite, Dr. D. A.
BFT #2798, 55pp., $5.50, Visuals on the Blood of the Lord Jesus Christ--For Overheads, Waite, Dr. D. A.
BFT #1804, C, $4.00, Why John MacArthur Downgrades The Blood Of Christ, Hymers, Dr. R. L.

Going To "Accredited" Schools

QUESTION #343

I am praying about going back to an accredited seminary to earn a Ph.D. in order to be eligible to teach in a Bible college or seminary. I have a Th.D. from an independent Baptist school, but it is unaccredited, so the world of academia does not recognize it. What I would like your help with is to ask which school to attend! Are there still some accredited schools out there that still hold to the fundamental, KJB position?

ANSWER #343

There are several issues here. (1) Are you sure you can get a job at a Bible College or Seminary that stands for the KJB and is a separatist school? (2) Are you sure they demand an "*accredited*" Ph.D.? (3) There might be accredited schools that you could get a Ph.D. from that might not be separatist and might not be KJB. I am not aware of too many schools that are both separatist and also defend the KJB. (4) Perhaps Ambassador Baptist College (which takes a partial stand for the TR and KJB though a teacher wrote a book wanting both positions to be friendly) might grant a Ph.D., but I'm not sure of it. (5) You might consider going to a purely secular school such as a State school that takes no stand on anything and get your degree. My Ph.D. is from Purdue University in Speech, for example. This field would be helpful in any area of ministry in the future.

Three of my degrees (A.B., M.A., and Ph.D.) were from accredited schools and two degrees (Th.M. and Th.D. from Dallas Seminary) were unaccredited. Yet I learned in that DTS school (though I would never send anyone to it now) theology, Hebrew, Greek, Church History, practical theology and preaching, and Bible all of which I use in my present ministry and people never worry about whether or not DTS was accredited when I attended. They take me for what I am and what I know, not what type of school I attended.

As the old saying goes, "*The Proof of the Pudding Is In The Eating*." That is, the thing that matters is not what name brand is on the pudding, but how does it taste when people eat it. There are many accredited graduates who are dunces and yet many un-accredited graduates that are smart and capable. And then there are those who have never gone to any school at all and yet have been honored by the Lord in their work such as Dr. H. A. Ironside and many others.

The Meaning Of Number "Ten"
QUESTION #344
We are having our Pastor's First Lady's, and family's Tenth Anniversary of service at our church. We would like to make it special using reference to the number "10." Is there a special meaning to "ten"?
ANSWER #344
Sorry, but I don't have information on the meaning of numbers. Various people have various ideas on these things. Harold Camping goes wild over various numbers and their meanings, but who knows if he is correct or not? I believe that giving special meanings of numbers in the Bible is pure speculation and should be avoided.

Christian "Orthodoxy"
QUESTION #345
Would you explain what "*Christian Orthodoxy*" means? Can you elaborate on what you consider areas of Christian Orthodoxy and what would be considered allowable areas of difference.

I'm still unclear about Charles Spurgeon. I've heard it said he was a five-point Calvinist. Then I've heard that he wasn't a Calvinist at all and never taught it. I heard from someone else that it sounded like some of what he said may have had some Calvinism in it.

ANSWER #345

Regarding Spurgeon first, he took both sides of Calvinism throughout his many writings. He on the one hand believed Christ died for the sins of the world and on the other hand believed strongly in the election of some and passing over of others. He was the same regarding the KJB and the English Revised Version (ERV). He quoted from both of them, but seemed to prefer the KJB more than the ERV. He is an anomaly.

Regarding "*Christian Orthodoxy*," generally speaking it is the opposite of "*Christian Heterodoxy*" which would be equated with "*Christian*" modernism, heresy, liberalism, and apostasy. Such denials of creation, the inerrancy of the Hebrew, Aramaic, and Greek originals, of the virgin birth of Christ, of His miracles, of His entire attributes of Deity, of his substitutionary Blood atonement of sinners, of Christ's Blood being able to forgive and to cleanse from sin, of Christ's bodily resurrection, of Christ's ability to forgive sins, of a literal heaven, of a literal lake of fire in Hell, of Christ's bodily ascension, or Christ's present seating at the Father's right hand in heaven, of His being the High Priests of the redeemed people, of His bodily return to this earth, and many other Biblical doctrines.

On the other hand, "*Christian Orthodoxy*" would affirm all of the above doctrines. Obviously, there are many doctrines about which people of "*Christian Orthodoxy*" have differing opinions, such as baptism, limited atonement, Calvinism, the rapture, premillennialism, Biblical separation, and other matters.

Why Sunday, Easter, & Christmas?

QUESTION #346

Most recently, the matter of why Church on Sunday and the Christmas and Easter "traditional" celebrations came up. What was discovered is that none of the above 3 items are Biblical but pagan in origin. This leaves me perplexed as to why America continues to conduct Church on Sunday and participate in Christmas and Easter.

ANSWER #346

You are correct that Christmas and Easter are pagan and God nowhere tells us to "celebrate" either of these heathen festivals. We believe in the Virgin birth of Christ and we believe in the substitutionary death for the sins of the world and the bodily resurrection of the Lord Jesus Christ.

> We worship the Lord on the first day of the week as the Bible indicates was the practice of the early church. While it is true that the name SUN day is pagan, it is still the first day of our week and thus we worship on that day despite the pagan name for the day.

"Through" Faith Or "By" Faith?
QUESTION #347
I honestly had overlooked two other items in the *Articles of Faith* after I sent my first email, one is probably just semantics. In the Bible For Today *Articles of Faith*, XVII, Section C says *"the new birth of the believer comes only through faith in Christ."* It says not *"by"* faith, but *"through"* faith. The reason this seems important to me is that revisions Bibles have changed the faith *"of"* God and Christ to faith *"in"* God and Christ. By saying we are saved by faith in Christ is like a work we have done.

> ### ANSWER #347
> Ephesians 2:8 states clearly that *"by grace are ye saved **through** faith."* (without any boasting or prideful motives). The word *"of"* is an objective genitive, rather than a subjective genitive. It means faith *"in"* Christ as an objective genitive. The hyper-Calvinists misinterpret this *"of"* as if God must give you the faith rather than the faith must come from the person who is trusting the Lord as Saviour. This is not a *"work."* It is genuine faith and trust in the finished work of the Lord Jesus Christ.

Election & Hyper-Calvinism
QUESTION #348
I'm half way through your book on Romans and had a question for you. Are predestination and election taught in the Bible? I'm a little confused over hyper-Calvinism.

ANSWER #348
Like many other terms, the word, *"Predestination,"* does not occur in our King James Bible, but *"Predestinate"* is used 2 times (Romans 8:29-30). *"Predestinated"* is used 2 times (Ephesians 1:5; 1:11)

"Election" is used 6 times (Romans 9:11; 11:5; 11:7, 28; 1 Thess. 1:4 and 2 Peter 1:10). *"Elected"* is used once (1 Peter 5:13). *"Elect"* is used 16 times: (Isa. 42:1; 45:4; 65:9; Matthew 24:24; 24:31; Mark 13:22; 13:27; Luke 18:7; Romans 8:33; Colossians 3:12; 1 Timothy 5:21; Titus 1:1; 1 Peter 1:2; 2:6; 2 John 1; 2 John 13).

I believe in all of these words, when interpreted properly, I believe that every born-again Christian has been *"predestinated to be conformed to the image of His Son*" (Romans 8:29). That is every believer's destiny or pre-destiny. That is how I define the Bible's teaching on "*predestination*."

> As far as "*election*" is concerned, I believe in it, as I said before, "*when it is interpreted properly.*" I believe in corporate election or choice. Just like God elected or chose Israel as a body, in like manner God elected or chose, before the foundation of the world, the Church as a body. Since the birth in this world of the Church which is Christ's Body at the day of Pentecost, every one who is genuinely saved and born-again becomes a member of that previously elected and chosen Body.

Though there are many other errors of the hyper-Calvinists, here are three of their major Biblical errors.

1. The hyper-Calvinists wrongly and unbiblically believe that the Lord Jesus Christ died only for the sins of a small group of people called the "*elect*," rather than, as the Bible clearly teaches, for the sins of the entire world, past, present, and future.

2. The hyper-Calvinists wrongly and unbiblically do not believe that everybody in the world has an opportunity genuinely to receive the Lord Jesus Christ as their Saviour and be saved. John 3:16 is very clear in showing their view to be false. It says that "*whosoever believeth*" in Him can be saved and have everlasting life. "*Whosoever*" cannot be limited to the "*elect*" only.

3. The hyper-Calvinists wrongly and unbiblically do not believe that God loves everybody. They teach that He loves only the "*elect*." This is also refuted by John 3:16 which says very clearly that "*God so loved the WORLD*" which includes everyone in the whole world, past, present and future.

What Is A Church Elder?

QUESTION #349

The part I don't understand is that there are Acts' verses which sound like there is more than one elder in that church. For instance, Acts 20:17 talks about calling the "*elders*" (plural) of the church (singular). Also, Acts 21:18 it talks about James and the "*elders*" at Jerusalem, which, if I understand correctly, was a very large church, so I just thought there were others there to help out because of the size. Was there a plurality of "*elders*" in the New Testament?

ANSWER #349

The "*elders*" could be plural if the churches were large. It could also be understood as plural to refer to smaller separate churches in the same town or area, each with one "*elder*" each.

The Presbyterians teach that there are "*teaching elders*" and "*ruling elders*." I explain a plurality of "*elders*" as referring to all the men being

Miscellaneous Questions   103

pastors/bishops/elders, including the assistants, one leading the church, another visiting, another with youth, another in education. Even though they are assistants, they can all still be called pastors/bishops/elders in accord with Acts and 1 Peter.

Expository Preaching In Churches
QUESTION #350

I wondered if you'd help me understand something. You have always stayed faithful to doing expository teachings. I've noticed that you start at the beginning of a particular book and preach straight through it, picking up each Sunday where you left off from the week before until you've finished that book and then move on to the next. Here is my question: What I have noticed over the years is a different approach in churches and ministers. For those that do use scripture, they will read a little scripture from the Bible and then expound on it, then the next week, they will go to a totally different book, read a little scripture and expound on it, then the next week, skip to another book and do the same. There seems to be no rhyme or reason to the picking and choosing of books here and there and the Scripture. Why is it that ministers do it in that way?

ANSWER #350

I believe that preaching and teaching the Bible verse by verse and chapter by chapter is the best way for a Pastor to fulfill His orders from the Lord to "*Preach the Word; Be instant, in season, out of season; Reprove, rebuke, exhort, with all longsuffering and doctrine*" (2 Timothy 4:2) The Pastors who preach topically or just pick a verse one Sunday and then another one the next Sunday are not "*preaching the Word*" in a consecutive manner so the saints can understand the "*whole counsel of God*." That is their preference certainly, but I do not think it is effective in the building up of the saints.

The reasons why they do this instead of expository preaching and teaching as I do are many: (1) Perhaps they don't want to spend the time it takes to study each verse of the particular book and preach and teach it. (2) Perhaps they have never been taught the Greek or Hebrew Words that underlie the Bible that they can call upon for further clarification of meanings of the words in the verses. (3) Perhaps they can't find other men's sermons that they can copy that preach in this manner and so content themselves with topical treatments or outlines they can steal from others who have thought them through. (4) Perhaps they cannot be original and fear a verse by verse method because they might come across some verses they either do not understand or that they don't believe can "preach" well enough. (5) Perhaps they feel that deep study of the Bible will drive people away and so they resort to a Rick

Warren superficial approach to preaching. (6) Perhaps their teachers where they went to school, either did not prepare them for verse by verse preaching, or even counseled them against it. (7) Perhaps there are many other reasons that you could suggest.

At the Dallas Theological Seminary (1948-1953), (the old Dallas, not the new one), we were taught to *"preach the Word"* and were given the tools to do it. I try my best to follow through on this training in the things of the Lord.

Churches And Elders?

QUESTION #351

Just wondered what your thoughts are on the following situation of a church with a pastor, two deacons, but no elders. Are all churches to have elders and deacons? Would there be any type problem that perhaps could develop with no elders in a church?

ANSWER #351

I believe the New Testament (and most Baptist churches agree) teaches that there should be deacons in every local church. But, according to the Bible, the pastor of each local church has a threefold description. He is the pastor. He is the elder. And he is the bishop. Acts 20:17-28 shows that *"elders"* are to "*shepherd*" or *"pastor"* and to take the "*oversight*" or be the *"bishops."* The same is taught in 1 Peter 5:1-2. Each local church has an *"elder"* as *"pastor."* If there are assistant *"pastors,"* there are assistant *elders* as well.

How To "Obey" Those Who "Rule"

QUESTION #352

In Hebrews 13:17 it says:

*"Obey them that have the rule over you, and submit yourselves: for they **watch for your souls**, as they that must **give account**, that they may do it with joy, and not with grief: for that is unprofitable for you."*

Do you know of an example for applying this verse? I haven't been able to fully submit to the leaders of churches I've attended because of their various false doctrines and/or practices. Is the Lord talking about obeying men who are obedient and faithful themselves?

Another Bible question related to pastors. If a pastor's daughter is rebellious and becomes illegitimately pregnant, would he be disqualified to be a pastor? Once she leaves his home (running away to get married) would he become qualified again?

Miscellaneous Questions

ANSWER #352

1. I believe those who "*watch for your souls*" should be "*obeyed*" insofar as they preach and teach clearly and faithfully the Words of God. They must "*give account*" to the Lord for what they do as leaders. I do not believe we have any necessity of "*obeying*" pastors or Christian teachers who teach heresy. I agree with you that these men must be obedient and faithful themselves.

Pastoral authority is Scriptural, but not pastoral dictatorship of the church members for every detail of their lives (as some pastors have assumed).

2. Titus 1:5-6 says:
"*For this cause left I thee in Crete, that thou shouldest set in order the things that are wanting, and ordain elders in every city, as I had appointed thee. If any be blameless, the husband of one wife,* **having faithful children not accused of riot or unruly**."

This is a command for pastors/bishops/elders to have "*faithful children not accused of riot or unruly.*"

1 Timothy 3:2-4 says:
"*A bishop then must be blameless, the husband of one wife, vigilant, sober, of good behaviour, given to hospitality, apt to teach; Not given to wine, no striker, not greedy of filthy lucre; but patient, not a brawler, not covetous;* **One that ruleth well his own house, having his children in subjection with all gravity**;"

This is also a clear command for pastors/bishops/elders to "*rule well his own house, having his children in subjection with all gravity.*" In view of God's Words, the pastor whose daughter has played the harlot while she has been living "*under his roof*" has disqualified himself for the ministry. I'm not so sure that he could qualify to come back into the ministry once the harlot daughter has left the house. His inability and flaws as a father live on.

1 Timothy 3:5 asks the question,
"(*For* **if a man know not how to rule his own house, how shall he take care of the church of God**?)"

Such a pastor has proved that he did "*not know how to rule is own house.*" Since that was firmly established by permitting his daughter to play the harlot, the next obvious question that Paul tells Pastor Timothy is "*how shall he take care of the church of God*"? The clear answer is that he cannot do it. Therefore, he should be put out of the ministry. I may be wrong in this, but I would doubt this pastor's qualifications. Perhaps he should get a job at a gas station or something.

CHAPTER IV
QUESTIONS ON THE KING JAMES BIBLE & VARIOUS BIBLE VERSIONS

Distortions on Bible Versions

QUESTION #353

Have you seen the video put out by the "Coalition for the Defense of the Scriptures" called *Fundamentalism and the Word of God*? I bought it at the BJU bookstore. I thought I was buying something that defended the KJV, but it doesn't. It was made in 1998.

ANSWER #353

Yes, I have not only seen this video, but I have answered it in my book, *Fundamentalist Distortions on Bible Versions* It is 80 pages, perfect bound (BFT #2928/P @ $7.00 + $5 S&H.) It has many distortions indeed.

Can 1769 KJB Be Called KJB?

QUESTION #354

I recently bought some *Defined King James Bibles*. On the opening page, it mentions that this is the Cambridge 1769 Text. Is there an article that you can point me to that explains the difference between the 1611 King James and the 1769 text? Can this 1769 text in effect still be called a King James Bible?

ANSWER #354

The 1769 is the latest updated edition of the 1611 including spelling, etc. "*Sinne*" is changed to "*sin*" and so on. Of the almost 800,000 words in the KJB, there are only about 1,000 or so minor changes which is a minute percentage. The 1769 KJB certainly can still be called the King James Bible.

Conversions And Modern Versions

QUESTION #355
What are your thoughts on the idea of "conversions to Christ" from modern versions? Do the liberal ideas flowing from Churches who have rejected the AV 1611 reflect false conversions?

ANSWER #355
Though it is possible for people to be saved from the improper translation that exists in some places of these perversions, once they are genuinely saved, they should switch to the full truth found in the KJB. If they do not switch to the KJB and continue in the perversions, I don't know how they can grow strong in all the doctrines since the new versions contain 356 doctrinal passages that are in error and have over 8,000 differences in the N.T. Greek Text and drop out 2,856 Greek N.T. Words. It is like going to garbage cans for food. Yes, some of it is good, but there is much lacking, and some will make you ill.

What's Wrong With The NKJV?

QUESTION #356
Will you please comment on your view of the NKJV and why.

ANSWER #356
I am opposed to the NKJV. I have given over 2,000 examples (in **BFT #1442 @ $10.00 + $5.00 S&H**) of dynamic equivalence, that is, adding to, subtracting from, or changing in other ways from the Hebrew, Aramaic, and Greek Words of God. I urge you to get that report. You can phone me if you wish for more details at **856-854-4747** and I can tell you more.

Differences In Various KJB Bibles

QUESTION #357
I am a convinced believer in the doctrine of the verbal plenary preservation of Scriptures and am a user of the KJB. This is a query I have regarding the KJB. I read that there are different or "types" of the KJV Bible, for example, the Oxford KJV, Cambridge KJV and Webster KJV. I would like to ask if there is a significant difference to these different types of KJV? Should we get too worried about any significant differences? Is there a type that can be called the "true" KJV Bible? One difference which I've noticed in different KJV Bibles is the capital "S" for 'spirit' in Gen 1:2. Some KJB's have it in small letter "spirit."

Questions on the KJB & Modern Versions

ANSWER #357

I am glad for your position on verbal plenary preservation of the original Words of the Bible. In our country there are so-called King James Bibles that change the 1769 edition in many ways, chiefly in spellings such as Elias vs. Elijah in the N.T., etc. I have found the Cambridge KJB to be closer to the 1769 than the Oxford KJB. They did a more careful job in reproducing that edition of the KJB. As you may know, both the Cambridge and the Oxford publishers in England are not supposed to alter the 1769. As for the "S" vs. "s," there are no capital letters used in the Bible in either the Hebrew or the Greek. It is a matter of interpretation as to whether the Holy Spirit or man's human spirit is meant. Our *Defined King James Bible* uses the Cambridge text because I believe it is the best KJB to use for many reasons.

Cambridge/Oxford KJB Differences

QUESTION #358

What are a few ways we can differentiate between a Cambridge KJB and an Oxford KJB? Also, with your view that the Cambridge KJB to be more faithful than the Oxford text, do you think that it is of any importance for KJB users to identify which KJB they are using and subsequently to use only the Cambridge version? Or do you think the differences in the two are not too significant and it is all right to use either one of the two?

ANSWER #358

Below are some of the differences between the Cambridge and the Oxford Bibles. Though some of the differences are small, yet small things matter and I would recommend our *Defined King James Bible* with Cambridge words to anyone who wants one. Dr. S. H. Tow has them in his bookstore I believe, hardback or genuine leather.

THREE DIFFERENCES BETWEEN OXFORD & CAMBRIDGE KING JAMES BIBLES:

(1) Jeremiah 34:16
   found in AV 1611, Hebrew, and Cambridge KJB
   16 But ye turned and polluted my name, and caused every man his servant, and every man his handmaid, whom **ye** had set at liberty at their pleasure, to return, and brought them into subjection, to be unto you for servants and for handmaids. (KJV)
   found in Oxford KJB & others
   Versus "whom **he** had set at liberty"

(2) 2 Chronicles 33:19
   found in AV 1611, Hebrew, and Cambridge KJB
   19 His prayer also, and how God was intreated of him, and all his **sin**, and his trespass, and the places wherein he built high places, and set up groves and graven images, before he was humbled: behold, they are written among the sayings of the seers. (KJV)
   found in Oxford KJB & others
   Versus "and all his **sins**"
(3) Nahum 3:16
   found in AV 1611, Hebrew, and Cambridge KJB
   16 Thou hast multiplied thy merchants above the stars of heaven: the cankerworm spoileth, and **flieth** away. (KJV)
   found in Oxford KJB & others
   Versus "and **fleeth** away"
   I have a more complete list compiled by Dean Lampman that I have in a PDF file (**CambOxfDifferences.102.pdf**). I can E-mail this PDF file to anyone who wishes it. Contact me at BFT@BibleForToday.org if you wish to get it.

Perverted Modern Bible Versions

QUESTION #359

I'm glad I have a KJB. What would be the best approach to show another person how perverted the other Bible versions are?

ANSWER #359

The best way to point out the deficiencies in the other versions is to point out their 356 doctrinal defective passages. In my book, *Defending the King James Bible* (**BFT #1594) @ $12.00 + $5.00 S&H),** Chapter V, I list 158 out of a total of 356 doctrinal passages where the new versions are in error. Doctrine should make a difference with a genuine Christian, but sometimes they do not care. All 356 doctrinal passages are detailed in almost 200 pages in Dr. Jack Moorman's book, *Early Manuscripts, Church Fathers, and the Authorized Version* (**BFT #3230 @ $20.00 + $7.00 S&H).**

What Does "Even" Mean?
QUESTION #360
John 1:12 says: "*But as many as received him, to them gave he power to become the sons of God, even to them that believe on his name:*"

In the clause, "*even to them that believe on his name*," does "*even*" have the same meaning today?

ANSWER #360
Though this word makes good sense here, "*even*" is in italics because it is not in the Greek text. The KJB supplied "*even*" to identify the fact that those who (1) "*received Him*" are the same group as those (2) who "*believe on his name.*" Both of these clauses identify those who "*become the sons of God.*"

"Neighbour" Or "Others"
QUESTION #361
Recently, I've been reading a book which has kindled an intense interest in Baptist history that I've not had in a long time. It has given rise in my mind to a point of curiosity: Have you or someone you know done any research and/or published any work that addresses the acceptance of the Authorized Version among Baptist people? Can the acceptance of the underlying Words of the Authorized Version (KJB) be traced in history?

ANSWER #361
I don't know of Baptists who have used the KJB in a book, but I know Spurgeon used the KJB, but also referred sometimes to the ERV or RV as it is called. I think the Baptists as a group, along with many other groups followed the TR from the Apostolic times to the present, or at least until 1881 when Westcott and Hort turned things around.

In my book, *Defending the King James Bible*, I list 37 historical links from the original New Testament Words to the modern times. I believe many of these "*links*" would include most, if not all, of the historic Baptist Churches. I am glad you are helped by the *Defending King James Bible*. Links # 10 and #11 deal with the Waldensians. They were a group holding to many doctrines also held by present-day Baptists.

Here are the 37 historical links for the Traditional Received Words of the New Testament. They are the Words on which the King James Bible is based. These links show that the King James Bible type of New Testament Words were accepted, not only by Baptists, but by all kinds of churches from the Apostolic times to the present.

The Thirty-Seven Historical Evidences Supporting the Textus Receptus. Here are the thirty-seven links in the chain of historical evidence to support the Received Text.

    a. Historical Evidences for the Received Text During the Apostolic Age (33--100 A.D.)

        (1)   All of the Apostolic Churches used the Received Text.

        (2)   The churches in Palestine used the Received Text.

        (3)   The Syrian Church at Antioch used the Received Text.

    b. Historical Evidences for the Received Text During the Early Church Period (100--312 A.D.).

    Dr. Scrivener and Dean Burgon both agree that, during the first 100 years after the New Testament was written, the greatest corruptions took place to the Received Text used by the early church. The B (Vatican) and Aleph (Sinai) manuscripts and the approximately forty-three allies which underlie the Westcott-and-Hort-type text were, I believe, the result of such corruptions. Some of the heretics which operated in this period were Marcion, (160 A. D.); Valentinus, (about 160 A. D.); Cyrinthus, (50-100 A. D.); Sabellius, (about 260 A. D.); and others.

        (4)   The Peshitta Syriac Version, (150 A. D., the second century.) This was based on the Received Text.

        (5)   Papyrus #66 used the Received Text.

        (6)   The Italic Church in Northern Italy (157 A. D.) used the Received Text.

        (7)   The Gallic Church of Southern France (177 A.D.) used the Received Text.

        (8)   The Celtic Church in Great Britain used the Received Text.

Why did all these have their Bibles based on the Received Text?--the churches in Italy, France, and Great Britain--why? Because those were the true Words of God, and they knew it. That was the Received Text. They lived in 150 A. D. The Bible was completed in 90-100 A. D. They had the originals right there in their hands and they based it on that which was pure, accurate, and preserved by God and by the Lord Jesus Christ Who preserves everything. These churches used this text and not any other. The heretics made most of the changes in the Received Text during this time; the greatest proportion of which, according to both Dr. Scrivener and Dean Burgon, were made during the first 100 years after they were originally written.

        (9)   Church of Scotland and Ireland used the Received Text.

        (10)   The Pre-Waldensian churches used the Received Text.

        (11)   The Waldensians (120 A. D. and onward) used the Received Text.

Questions on the KJB & Modern Versions 113

   c. **Historical Evidences for the Received Text During the Byzantine Period (312--1453 A.D.)**

   (12) The Gothic Version of the 4th century used the Received Text.
   (13) Codex W of Matthew in the 4th or 5th century used the Received Text.
   (14) Codex A in the Gospels (in the 5th century) used the Received Text.
   (15) The vast majority of extant New Testament manuscripts all used the Received Text. This includes about 99% of them, or about 5,210 of the 5,255 MSS preserved by the Aland's in Munster, Germany as of 1967.
   (16) The Greek Orthodox Church used the Received Text. We don't agree with many of their doctrines or practices, but that entire church for over 1,000 years has used the Received Text. Why? They know the Greek language. They're Greeks. Even though they are modern Greeks, they use the New Testament that is based upon the Received Text because it is the Words of God, and they know it.
   (17) The present Greek Church still uses the Received Text. When Mrs. Waite and I were in Israel, we visited the church which is supposed to be on the place where Jesus was born, the Church of the Nativity. They have a big Church built on the site. It doesn't look anything like the original place, I am certain. I don't even think it is on the proper place. They have commercialized it. In Jerusalem, they have Christ born in various places, crucified in various places, and buried in several places. In the Church of the Nativity, Christ's supposed birth place, we met a Greek Orthodox priest. I said to him, "You're a member of the Greek Orthodox clergy, is that right?" He said, "Yes," and then told us his name. I said, "You have a New Testament you use, don't you?" "Oh, yes," he said. I asked, "Which text do you use? Are you familiar with the so-called Westcott-and-Hort-type-text?" "Oh, yes," he said, "We use the Received Text; we have no confidence at all in the Westcott and Hort text." That was interesting. The Greek Orthodox Church still goes back to this text that underlies the KING JAMES BIBLE.

   d. **Historical Evidences for the Received Text During the Early Modern Period (1453--1831 A.D.)**

   (18) The churches of the Reformation all used the Received Text.
   (19) The Erasmus Greek New Testament (1516) used the Received Text.
   (20) The Complutensian Polyglot (1522) used the Received Text. A Roman Catholic Cardinal named Ximenes, edited it, yet it was based, not on

the texts which most Roman Catholic Bibles used, the Westcott and Hort text, but on the Received Text.

(21) Martin Luther's German Bible (1522) used the Received Text.

(22) William Tyndale's Bible, (1525), used the Received Text. Tyndale was a great Bible translator who was martyred because of his Bible translation.

(23) The French Version of Oliveton (1535) used the Received Text.

(24) The Coverdale Bible (1535) used the Received Text.

(25) The Matthews Bible (1537) used the Received Text.

(26) The Taverners Bible (1539) used the Received Text.

(27) The Great Bible (1539-41) used the Received Text.

(28) The Stephanus Greek New Testament (1546-51) used the Received Text.

(29) The Geneva Bible (1557-60) used the Received Text.

(30) The Bishops' Bible (1568) used the Received Text.

(31) The Spanish Version (1569) used the Received Text.

(32) The Beza Greek New Testament (1598) used the Received Text. That is the Greek text that the KING JAMES BIBLE was based on, using the 1598, 5th edition of Beza.

(33) The Czech Version (1602) used the Received Text.

(34) The Italian Version of Diodati (1607) used the Received Text.

(35) The KING JAMES BIBLE (1611) used the Received Text.

(36) The Elzevir Brothers' Greek New Testament (1624) used the Received Text.

(37) The Received Text in the New Testament is the Received Text--the text that has survived in continuity from the beginning of the New Testament itself. It is the only accurate representation of the originals we have today!

> In fact, it is my own personal conviction and belief, after studying this subject since 1971, that the Words of the Received Greek and Masoretic Hebrew texts that underlie the King James Bible are the very Words which God has preserved down through the centuries, being the exact Words of the originals themselves. As such, I believe they are inspired Words. I believe they are preserved Words. I believe they are inerrant Words. I believe they are infallible Words. This is why I believe so strongly that any valid translation must be based upon these original language texts, and these alone!

Clarifying The King James Bible
QUESTION #362
Should I say that the King James Bible was faithfully translated by godly scholars, to give us God's Words faithfully rendered in English? Thanks for the clarification.
ANSWER #362
You have well stated it. The subtitle for my book, *Defending the King James Bible* (**BFT #1594** @ $12.00 + $7.00 S&H) calls our King James Bible *"God's Words Kept Intact In English."* This is because its translation, made from the proper Hebrew, Aramaic, and Greek Words is true, reliable, and accurate.

The KJB & "Derived Inspiration"
QUESTION #363
The King James Version is the only English version I can trust. But does the King James Version have a *"derived inspiration"* from its Hebrew, Aramaic, and Greek Words from which it was translated?
ANSWER #363
I am glad that you are now on the side of the King James Bible and its underlying Hebrew, Aramaic, and Greek Words. As far as saying the KJB has *"derived inspiration,"* I do not agree. I believe the Bible limits the terms, "*inspiration*," "*inspiration of God*," "*given by inspiration of God*," or "*God-breathed*" (THEOPNEUSTOS) to the Hebrew, Aramaic, and Greek Words originally given by God in that once-for-all process. Those Words have been verbally and plenarily preserved in the Hebrew, Aramaic, and Greek Words underlying the King James Bible. In taking this position, we don't have to define "*inspiration*" in two different ways, one for the Hebrew, Aramaic, and Greek Words, and another for translations of those Words in English, German, Italian, French, Spanish, Chinese, or other languages.

Chapter And Verse Divisions
QUESTION #364
What do you say to someone who says "I don't like the chapter and verse divisions in the King James Version?"
ANSWER #364
Let this person look at the verse divisions in any other version if he doesn't like those in the KJB. Try the NIV, NASV, RSV, NRSV, NKJV, ESV, etc., and he will find the same chapter and verse divisions. If my memory serves

me, these divisions were made in the N.T. in about 1550 A.D. by Stephens. These divisions assist us in identifying the same verse or chapter in any version of the Bible. The chapter and verse divisions are not inspired of God. They are man-made for facility in referring to the Words of God in N.T. Greek and the translation of those verses into English, Spanish, French, and other languages.

Changes In N.T. Name Spellings

QUESTION #365

Why are certain words spelled differently in some Bibles that are called King James Versions? How do I find which spellings are correct?

ANSWER #365

You can look up certain verses to find out how some proper names and other words are spelled. For example:

Look at Matthew 3:3 and all other places where Esaias is found and see if it is wrongly changed to Isaiah.

Look at Matthew 13:14 and all other places where Elias is found and see if it is wrongly changed to Elijah.

Look at Matthew 2:17 and all other places where Jeremy is found and see if it is wrongly changed to Jeremiah.

Look at Hebrews 4:8 where Jesus is found and see if it is wrongly changed to Joshua.

Look at Genesis 11:3 and all other places where throughly is found and see if it is wrongly changed to thoroughly.

These are just a few of the spelling changes that are not true to the King James Bible. There may be many other things as well. Names in the Cambridge edition of the King James Bible (like our *Defined King James Bible*) are proper transliterations of the Greek New Testament and are not changed to the Hebrew Old Testament transliteration.

Going To Hell For Not Using KJB?

QUESTION #366

Without trying to sound contentious or facetious, may I ask one question? I am not trying to be facetious. Do you think people that don't use the KJV are going to hell?

ANSWER #366

Though I firmly believe that the KJB is the only accurate English Bible translation from the proper Hebrew, Aramaic, and Greek Words, and I recommend to use it, preach it, believe it, and obey it, the using of it or not using it does not determine whether or not a person is going to Hell. Hell is the destiny of everyone who has not genuinely received the Lord Jesus Christ as their Saviour. Though people should use the King James Bible, going to Heaven or Hell depends on what people do with the Lord Jesus Christ, not on what Bible they may or may not use.

Number Of Words & Verses In KJB

QUESTION #367

Could you please help me know the exact number of words in the KJV? I have written down a count (which I obtained years ago) as follows:
773,692 words
31,173 verses
1,189 chapters
66 books

ANSWER #367

In our *Defined King James Bible*, we used the data from the Bible my high school janitor gave me when he led me to the Lord in October of 1944. If you note in our early pages, this is what we have:
NT has 27 books, 266 Chapters,   7,957 Verses, 180,751 Words
OT has 39 books, 929 Chapters, 23,144 Verses, 610,577 Words
        66 books, 1195 Chapters 31,101 Verses   791,328 Words

Check my addition and Check our Defined KJB to see if these add up all right. Some man years ago had different figures, but these are the ones we have.

"Worship" Of The KJB?--A Smear

QUESTION #368

What is your answer to those who might say we *"worship the KJB"*?

ANSWER #368

The phrase "*worship KJB*" should be understood by your foes and your friends. This is a smear against those of us who stand for the KJB. We do not "*worship the KJB*," but the KJB is an English yardstick by which to detect in other translations around the world defections from the MT and/or the TR. It is a reliable yardstick of measure because (1) it is founded on the proper inspired, inerrant, preserved, Hebrew, Aramaic, and Greek Words and (2) because it is an accurate translation of those Words into the English language. For details, we can always check the original Words that have been preserved.

In The N.T., "Jesus" Or "Joshua"

QUESTION #369

What is the reason for the reference to "*Jesus*" in Acts 7:45? Shouldn't that be "*Joshua*"?

ANSWER #369

Though it refers to "Joshua," the KJB translators in Acts 7:45 transliterated the Greek Word, IHSOUS, correctly as "*Jesus.*" The Hebrew Word for "*Joshua*" means Saviour and the Greek Word for "*Jesus*" also means Saviour. The KJB is accurate to the Greek text.

What Does "Inspiration" Mean?

QUESTION #370

When Paul sent his letter to the Ephesians, some scribe sat down and made a "*copy*" (letter for letter, jot and tittle) of that letter. Can that "*copy*" be called "*inspired Scripture*" or not? What is your position on the Greek and Hebrew "*copies*" that were made during the time of the original writings?

ANSWER #370

I believe the term "*inspired Scripture*" might be misleading. It might be taken to mean that those Words were given by the **process** of inspiration in the same that the original Words were given. This is a false position. It seems that it would confuse the originals with the copies. This would be a serious confusion and error. I believe the Words in accurate copies of the original Hebrew, Aramaic, and Greek Words can be called "*inspired Words*" because they are accurate copies of the Words that were given by the **process** of God's "*inspiration*" and breathing them out. I believe the Hebrew, Aramaic, and Greek Words underlying the King James Bible are the preserved copies of the originals themselves.

The Evidence Bible

QUESTION #371

Can you tell me anything about *The Evidence Bible* by Ray Comfort (Compiler) that uses quotes from the Amplified Bible?

ANSWER #371

http://www.jesus-is-savior.com/Bible/the_evidence_bible.htm is a LINK that is critical of The Evidence Bible by Ray Comfort. Why not look this up, read it, and evaluate it for yourself. I have not personally looked at it.

KJB--Imperfect Tense As Aorist?
QUESTION #372
I have a general question I would like to ask. We are finding that the King James translators often translate the imperfect tense as a normal aorist tense. I would like to know the reasoning behind this so we can apply that same criteria to what we do here.

ANSWER #372
The English can often be ambiguous on this point. I ran into the same question in helping in a French translation of the Gospel of John. In English it is not always possible to detect the difference between the imperfect and the simple past tense by the form of the verb. We don't have a separate form for the imperfect. We have to pick that up by either checking the Greek or Hebrew or by the context if possible. This is why it is important to check the tense of the Greek verb when doing exegesis or translation.

Are There Errors In The KJB?
QUESTION #373
There are three questions that I have.
1) Are there any errors in our present KJB?
2) There were so many revisions of the KJB, which one should we honour?
3) Is the Beza 1598 5th edition the only edition we should use when we translate?

ANSWER #373
(1) I don't believe there are any *"translation errors"* in the King James Bible. By this, I mean they used at least one valid rule of Hebrew, Aramaic, or Greek grammar in their translation. I also mean that they used at least one of the valid meanings of the Hebrew, Aramaic, or Greek Words in their translation. It must be remembered that the 1611 meaning of the English words is not always the same meaning used currently.

(2) I think we should use the 1769 edition which is now used by both Oxford and Cambridge University presses. Our *Defined King James Bible* is the Cambridge 1769 edition. The Cambridge edition is more accurate than that of Oxford.

(3) I believe that all translations in any language of the world should be made from the same Hebrew, Aramaic, and Greek original language Words used by our King James Bible. That would be the Masoretic Hebrew Old Testament Words and Beza's 5th edition, 1598, Greek Words as printed in *Scrivener's Annotated Greek New Testament* (**BFT #1670** @ $35.00 + $7.00

S&H).

> My personal position, based upon both facts and faith, is that the specific Hebrew, Aramaic, and Greek Words underlying the King James Bible are copies of God's original Words. As such, they are inspired, preserved, inerrant, and infallible Words.

Are Translations "Inspired"?

QUESTION #374

I did have a couple questions about your view on inspiration. (1) Is the KJB a 100% accurate copy of the original inspired manuscripts? (2) Could you say the KJB is inspired because it is His preserved Word? (3) Would not inspiration be a part of preservation?

ANSWER #374

1. No, it is not. I would say it this way: The translated words of the King James Bible would be accurate **translations** of God's inspired, preserved, inerrant Hebrew, Aramaic and Greek Words, but they are not those Hebrew, Aramaic, and Greek Words themselves.
2. No, you could not say that. In the Biblical sense, "given by inspiration of God" (2 Timothy 3:16) comes from THEOPNEUSTOS. That means literally "*God-breathed*." No translation was "*God-breathed*," therefore, no translation can be called "*inspired*." The use of that term for translations is a serious theological error. The King James Bible preserves, in accurately translated English, the Hebrew, Aramaic and Greek Words which God Preserved verbally and fully.
3. Inspiration is not a part of preservation. It has nothing whatsoever to do with preservation. Inspiration was a miracle operation of God whereby, through God the Holy Spirit, He gave human writers the Hebrew, Aramaic, and Greek Words of the Bible. That inspiration will never again be repeated at any time or in any place, or in any translation. Preservation has to do with God's preserving down to our present day His inspired Hebrew, Aramaic, and Greek Words.

Modern Versions & Salvation

QUESTION #375

The Administrative Elder in my church is of the opinion that no matter what flaws have been created in the NIV, people are still being led to Christ through this book. How do I answer that?

ANSWER #375

It might be that some are being "*led to Christ*" by using the NIV. I have no way of proving this either right or wrong. If they are saved, and continue using the NIV, they will become people with spiritual anorexia whose skinny spiritual souls can hardly manage to keep on going and growing. Here's what I mean by this.

    1. Their NIV Greek New Testament has over 8,000 erroneous Greek differences with the traditional Greek Words that underlie the King James Bible.

    2. They have a Greek New Testament that is 2,886 words shorter than the traditional Words underlying the King James Bible.

    3. They have a New Testament that has 356 doctrinal passages that are in doctrinal error.

    4. They have (by my actual count) over 8,653 additions, subtractions, or other translation changes from the Hebrew, Aramaic, and Greek Words.

    5. They also have many doctrinal terms that have been removed from the NIV such as "*propitiation*," "*mercy seat*," and others.

> They might be saved, but they cannot depend upon a version that is flawed in so many ways. By using this NIV perversion, they make God a liar when compared to our King James Bible which has everything in place without doctrinal errors, without missing words, without added words, without changed words and with all of its doctrinal terms intact.

The Darby And Kelly Translations
QUESTION #376

The question of which Bible we should use has only recently been an issue for me. There is no greater. There is no more important subject and for time and eternity. We need to be 100% sure that the Hebrew and Greek that underlie a translation of the Bible is exactly what the blessed God has said.

In recent times, I have been using what is called a new translation by John Nelson Darby. I have the edition with his full textual notes on how and why he departed from the TR. I know that Mr. Darby, as he did his work, did so in the fear of God. He was completely persuaded that he was dealing with the very Word of God.

I also have Mr William Kelly's work on the Revised Version. It is a very helpful examination of the Greek text on where, in his judgment, they were right or wrong.

If I understand your position correctly would I be right in saying that you would reject the sober godly and reverential judgment of the above two men through whom to this day many of the saints of God are indebted to for the light, instruction, and blessing that our faithful risen Lord recovered for his assembly? Is this your position?

> **ANSWER #376**
>
> I know that Darby was with the Plymouth Brethren and that <u>he was a godly man, but I believe he was deceived by the Vatican and Sinai manuscripts in all too many places in his translation.</u> Kelly was the same, though I don't know as much about Kelly. Darby followed Tregelles who was also one of the Plymouth Brethren who was deceived by the unbelievers like Griesbach, Lachmann, and Tischendorf who followed wholly the Gnostic Critical Greek Text.
>
> I believe God promised to preserve His Hebrew, Aramaic, and Greek Words. I believe, for many reasons, having studied this matter since 1970, that the Hebrew, Aramaic, and Greek Words underlying the King James Bible are the exact Words of the originals themselves. My personal conclusion on this is based both on facts and on faith. Others can disagree if they wish, but this is my conclusion.
>
> I urge you to get my book, *DEFENDING THE KING JAMES BIBLE* (BFT #1594 @ $12.00 + $7.00 S&H) if you want to know my full view of the KJB defense.

Why Not Use Modern Versions?

QUESTION #377

Is God still using the modern translations, even though we know what has happened with their underlying Greek and Hebrew Words? Why are there certain men saying not to use them?

ANSWER #377

It is hard to come up with an answer that can satisfy everyone. To the extent that in these modern perversions that they have translated the right Hebrew, Aramaic, and Greek Words properly, these positions might be used of the Lord.

> However, it must be faced that (1) the Greek NT of these perversions have over 8,000 differences with the Words underlying the King James Bible; (2) Their Greek NT is 2,886 Words shorter than the KJB NT; (3) Their Greek NT has 356 doctrinal passages that are in error.

In summary, I would not trust any of these modern perversions with the eternal souls of men and women because they would be getting a very different New Testament with many doctrinal perversions contained therein. The additional problem is that these people do not know where these errors are found or which doctrines are absent from or perverted in their modern versions.

New Versions "Another Gospel"?
QUESTION #378
When the preacher is preaching from a corrupted version, is he preaching another gospel and another Christ? If so, how can people be saved?
ANSWER #378
A person can be saved if the preacher or other Christian person uses only verses that are true in the modern versions. For example, John 3:16 is somewhat clear, though not completely. The same is true of John 14:6; Acts 4:12; John 3:18; John 3:36; Romans 3:23; Romans 6:23 and some others. He cannot, however, use the false translation of John 6:47 that leaves out "*on me,*" nor can he use many, many others of the over 356 doctrinal passages that are in error in the new versions.

Albigenses, Darby, & "Hell"
QUESTION #379
About Albigenses or Cathari, most of current information from internet called them heretics. But William Jones, in his *History of the Christian Church*, has written the most positive position about them. I don't know. What do you think?

We met a French brother who used Darby's French and English Bible. I showed him *The Doctored New Testament*. When I showed him Matthew16:18, he said "*the gates of hell*" is translated in the KJV, but it is not in the Received Text. What do you think about Darby's Bible?
ANSWER #379
The Albigenses and Cathari were not heretics. Though they might have had some doctrines we differ with, I believe they were indeed forerunners of many of the principles now believed by the Bible-believing Baptists.

> As far as Matt. 16:18 not having the "*gates of hell,*" he is wrong again. The Greek word is HADES and it is properly translated in our KJB as HELL, though it is not the only word for HELL. GEHENNA is another word that is translated HELL. The new versions are cowards when they come to the Greek word HADES. They transliterate, but do not translate it. HELL is a valid translation of the Greek word, HADES.

As far as my opinion on the Darby translation is concerned, let me say this. Though some of Darby is based on the Textus Receptus (TR), much is not. It is based on the Gnostic Critical Greek Text. If you have my book called *THE CASE FOR THE KING JAMES BIBLE* (**BFT #83** @ **$7.00 + $4.00 S&H**) on pages 61 and 62, I have a list of 44 New Testament and Greek versions which compare 162 verses which should use TR's words in all 162 verses; but they do not. There is listed the number of parts of verses that are omitted in each of the 44 versions and then the percentage of parts of verses omitted in them. The #1 version, which is the farthest removed from the TR is the RSV of 1881 with 158 of 162 where parts of verses are omitted. The #44 version, which is the closest to the TR is the King James Bible with 0 of the 162 verses where parts of the verses are omitted.

In this list of 44 New Testament verses, the Darby translation is #34 where 75 of the 162 have parts of the verses omitted. That is far too many for me. Therefore, I would not use the Darby translation or recommend others to use it regardless of the fact that he was one of the Plymouth Brethren. He was no doubt influenced by Samuel Tregelles who was also a member of the Plymouth Brethren, who, though he was a saved man, he was sold out to the false Westcott and Hort Gnostic Critical Greek Text.

ASV, ERV And The KJB Comparisons

QUESTION #380

Do we have any comparison done between the ASV and the KJB or ERV and the KJB?

ANSWER #380

No, I have not made such a comparison nor do I know of any available. The ASV of 1901 and the ERV of 1881 are virtually identical in both the OT and NT. I recommend you get an OLD EDITION of Strong's Exhaustive Concordance where he has made note of the DIFFERENCES between the KJB and the ERV.

Debating BJU Pastors On TR

QUESTION #381

I have been attending a Fundamental Baptist Church where the pastor preaches from the KJV but accepts other versions (NKJV, NASV). He graduated from BJU in the 1980s and now his children go there as well as other young people from the church. Do you think there is any chance of convincing him his stand is wrong or would it be best to separate from this church? It is a problem because my wife, her sister and niece also attend this church with her two little girls. I have resisted joining the church and am faced with "What do I do with my Family?"

ANSWER #381

I believe it is a waste of your time to attempt to convince this BJU graduate to leave his Alma Mater's position on the Greek text of the N.T. and the various Bible perversions. Do what you will, but you will see there is a stone wall between your position on the KJB and that of your pastor. You have but one of three positions to take: (1) leave the church and go to a church that stands for the King James Bible and its underlying Hebrew, Aramaic, and Greek Words; (2) stay in the church and swallow hard and grin and bear it, subjecting your family and children to this error; (3) listen to our services at the Bible For Today Baptist Church over the internet at BibleForToday.org by clicking on the **BROWN BOX** each Sunday at 10 a.m., 1:30 p.m., and Thursday at 8:00 p.m. (Eastern) by means of our church's STREAMING VIDEOS until you can find a good and sound KJB church.

Should New Versions Be Trusted?
QUESTION #382

There are many English translations. And I know that KJV's New Testament is based on the TR. What can you say about the NKJV? Or the NASV? Can those Bibles be trusted? My English is not good. That is why the King James Bible is a little bit hard to understand for me.

ANSWER #382

The NASV, NIV, RSV, NRSV, ESV, NKJV, and many others cannot be trusted. The only English translation you can trust is the King James Bible. Since you have difficulty in understanding some of the words in the King James Bible, you should get one of our *DEFINED KING JAMES BIBLES*. This will help you with uncommon English words which have been defined accurately for you in the footnotes.

Any Faithful Modern Translations?
QUESTION #383

We believe that God has preserved His Words in the Traditional Texts and the Authorized King James Version, but I occasionally get questions similar to the following: "*Does a modern-day English version exist that is faithfully translated from the Textus Receptus and Masoretic Text*"?

ANSWER #383

I know of no "*modern-day*" English version that is a faithful translation from the TR and MT. The King James Bible is the only English Bible that does this.

It is not that this is not **possible**, but due to the leanings of modern publishers, the false textual views of would-be translators, the poor scholarship and ability of these translators, and the modern translating technique of dynamic equivalency rather than verbal and formal equivalence, it is not **probable** that such a translation will be made. I would suggest to your students that they get our *DEFINED KING JAMES BIBLE* which brings the KJB up to date by defining accurately uncommon words.

Is NKJV Closer To TR Than KJB?

QUESTION #394

Barbara Aho of www.watch.pair.com has suggested that the NKJV is closer to the Textus Receptus than the KJV. Can you give me some feedback on this?

ANSWER #384

It depends on which Textus Receptus you mean. If she means Stephens 1550 (as used in Berry's Interlinear), that varies in over 150 or 200 places I am told. If you use the TR from which the KJB was taken (Beza's 5th edition, 1598), the variations are few. Dr. Frederick Scivener's Greek Text is the TR that exactly underlies the KJB with no variations.

So far as the NKJV being dependable and reliable, I have found over 2,000 examples where the NKJV either adds, subtracts, or changes from the underlying Textus Receptus or OT Masoretic Words. This is available in print as BFT #1442 and can be ordered on www.BibleForToday.org as below. The NKJV cannot be trusted as a reliable translation from the Hebrew, Aramaic, and Greek Words underlying the KJB.

Item #	Category	Author
OP1442	BFT Office Publications	Waite, Dr. D. A.

New King James Version Analyzed (Cf. #1465 Tract) Gift: **$10.00** +**$6.00 S&H**

What About The Portuguese Bible?
QUESTION #385
Do you support the use of this Portuguese Bible? The Almeida Corrigida Fiel 1995 Trinitarian Bible Society Brazil? Is this a pure Bible following the TR? What information do you have on it?
ANSWER #385
The TBS Portuguese N.T. is the best to date, but, according to my friend, Col. Jose Pedro Almeida of Brazil, it has several hundred places where it should be corrected. Why not write him and ask him about these details. His present e-mail address is: jotaetil@hotmail.com. His name is Col. Jose Pedro Almeida. You can ask him for his comments. Portuguese is his mother tongue. He also knows the Greek New Testament language as well. He is a valued member of the Dean Burgon Society's Advisory Council. As such, he stands with us in our position on the Hebrew, Aramaic, and Greek Words underlying the KJB and on the KJB itself.

Analysis Of NKJV For Laymen
QUESTION #386
Is *The New King James Version Analyzed* (**BFT #1442**) suitable for the laymen, or is it only for scholars?
ANSWER #386
This book can be used by scholars as well as lay people. The differences are not only in Greek from Matthew through Revelation but also in English. You can see the differences where they show up in English and compare these places to any language translation in the world to see the errors. Over 356 of these places involve doctrinal passages.

How Often For The Lord's Supper?
QUESTION #387
I have been in my Baptist church every Sunday and it has not had the Lord's Supper once. I would also like to participate in the Lord's Supper once in a while. How often should churches celebrate the Lord's Supper?
ANSWER #387
As far as the Lord's Supper is concerned, I have found that many churches in California that I have had contact with do not believe in having it each month, but only once a quarter, or even once a year. I find that strange, but that is their custom. Our church celebrates the Lord's Table the first Sunday of each

month. Other churches have different schedules for this, all the way from once a week, once a month, once a quarter, twice a year, or once a year. Some of those who are hyperdispensationalists do not celebrate this ordinance at all.

CHAPTER V
QUESTIONS ON MARRIAGE, DIVORCE, REMARRIAGE & WOMEN'S ISSUES

No Deacon Divorce/Remarriage
QUESTION #388

I feel confident that one argument I'll have to respond to is that I Tim. 3:12 is written in the present tense. The phrase reads, Let the deacons be the *"husbands of one wife."* Most likely, I'll hear an argument such as this:

"We should only examine a man in light of his current and present marriage relationship. If he was married and got divorced before he was saved, but has since been married again and is today faithful to that wife, he meets the qualifications set forth in I Tim. 3:12."

I've already considered responding by saying that in God's eyes the man has two wives. My only concern here is that I'm sure the response to me will be

"If the divorce was lawful in accordance to Paul's instructions in I Cor. whether before he was saved or after he was saved, God does not recognize the man as having two wives."

Do you have any advice on how to respond to those two lines of thought that I may have to contend with?

ANSWER #388

1. The usual genius of the Greek present tense is CONTINUOUS ACTION. Let the deacon be CONTINUOUSLY (PAST, PRESENT, AND FUTURE) *"the husband of one wife."* No matter whether he was saved or lost during a divorce and remarriage.

2. There is NO Scriptural reason for divorce and remarriage which argument #2 presupposes and many teach. Remarriage can occur Scripturally

> with God's blessing only upon the death of the mate.
> Mark 10:11-12 is clear on this.
> Luke 16:18 is clear on this
> Romans 7:2-3 is clear on this
> 1 Corinthians 7:10-11 is clear on this

Restoration Of Marriage

QUESTION #389

I have been standing for the restoration of my marriage now for almost three years. I have a question about the state of my wife's soul. My question is this: Can my wife be saved in the state of adultery that she is now living in? She has now remarried. I would appreciate your comments from the Bible.

ANSWER #389

Any lost sinner can be saved by personal, genuine, and heart-felt faith in the Lord Jesus Christ. Although all of these things are displeasing to the Lord, since they have the flesh nature, saved people are capable of all sorts of "*works of the flesh*" as outlined in Galatians 5:19-21. This includes "*adultery.*" I don't know your wife's heart. Only God does. He alone knows whether she is a lost, hell-bound falsely professing "*Christian*" and not genuinely saved, or whether she is genuinely God's child but acting after the dictates of her flesh in a carnal, sinful way like the devil's child in disobedience to the Lord. Only our God knows the real answer. I do know this. Marriage is for life and "*until death us do part.*" I guess the real question is, can a genuine born-again Christian ever lose his or her salvation? The answer is "No." Can a genuine born-again Christian ever walk after the "*works of the flesh*" (including adultery)? Yes, sad to say. We cannot be saved by good works and we cannot be lost by bad works.

No Divorce & Remarriage

QUESTION #390

A Christian friend of mine wants to divorce her husband. She says that it is clear that the Bible teaches it is all right for her to divorce her husband because her husband has committed adultery. She says that if she does not divorce her husband, she will lose the chance of remarrying and getting financial support for herself and her daughter. Her husband has been away from the family for about a year already. Is her interpretation of Matthew 19:9 correct? "*And I say unto you, Whosoever shall put away his wife, except (it) be for fornication, and shall marry another, committeth adultery: and whoso marrieth her which is put away doth commit adultery.*" In other words, is fornication a just cause for divorce? Also, according to this verse, if she

Questions on Marriage, Re-Marriage, & Women

divorces her husband because her husband has committed fornication, Is it all right for her to remarry?

ANSWER #390

I am sorry that your friend (1) wants to divorce her husband rather than to seek to reconcile with him somehow, and (2) that she wants to re-marry against the clear teachings of the Words of God. Here are some very clear Bible verses

1. Romans 7:2-3 is very clear.

7:2 *For the woman which hath an husband is bound by the law to her husband so long as he liveth; but if the husband be dead, she is loosed from the law of her husband.*

3 So then if, while her husband liveth, she be married to another man, **she shall be called an adulteress***: but if her husband be dead, she is free from that law; so that she is no adulteress, though she be married to another man.*

2. 1 Corinthians 7:10-11 is clear:

7:10 *And unto the married I command, yet not I, but the Lord,* **Let not the wife depart from her husband***:*

11 But and **if she depart, let her remain unmarried, or be reconciled to her husband***: and let not the husband put away his wife.*

3. 1 Corinthians 7:39 is clear:

7:39 *The wife is bound by the law as long* **as her husband liveth***; but if her husband be dead, she is at liberty to be married to whom she will; only in the Lord.*

4. Mark 10:11-12 is clear:

Mark 10:11 *And he saith unto them, Whosoever shall put away his wife, and marry another, committeth adultery against her.*

12 And **if a woman shall put away her husband, and be married to another, she committeth adultery***.*

5. Luke 16:18 is clear:

Luke 16:18 **Whosoever putteth away his wife, and marrieth another, committeth adultery***: and whosoever marrieth her that is put away from her husband committeth adultery.*

The lady is not interpreting Matthew 19:9 correctly. This speaks of those in the Jewish families who were "*espoused*" but not yet married. Such espousals must be broken by "*divorce*." This was the case of "*fornication*" before being married, but "*espoused*." This is not the case today of "*marriage*" which is not the Jewish "*espousal*." Mark 10 and Luke 16 are clear and there are no "exceptions." Your prayer for her to return to her husband is well founded.

Divorce & ReMarriage Battles
QUESTION #391

Recently, it was decided that a revision of our Church Constitution should be made. I am one of four members assigned to completing this project before it is presented to the church for its approval or disapproval. In our last meeting we ran into a snag. The issue of divorce and deacons came up which led to a discussion of I Timothy 3:12. I hold the view that I Timothy 3:12 does not allow for a divorced man to hold the office of deacon. However, this is not the view held by another member of our committee. Instead, she feels that the phrase, *"Husbands of one wife"* has reference only to polygamy.

She made the comment that the Greek word used for one in that phrase likewise has reference to polygamy. I have studied every commentator available to me and found them to be of mixed opinions. I have read, Matthew Henry, John Gill, John Wesley, Oliver Greene, the JFB Commentary, Matthew Poole, H.A. Ironside, and Kenneth Wuest. The first four seem to think that the phrase in question deals with both polygamy and divorce. However, the last three seem to restrict the verse to polygamy only. Ironside seems to go so far as not holding divorce against a man as far as him being qualified for the office of deacon. John MacArthur does as well, but I don't have a lot of confidence in his opinion anyway.

As I'm sure you're aware, many commentators hold to the opinion that if divorce was acted upon for the lawful reasons mentioned by Paul in I Cor, this does not disqualify a man from the office of deacon. There are many who use Scofield as an example.

Your opinion on this issue would be very appreciated by me on two levels.

1) As a pastor and Bible Teacher, your doctrinal interpretation on the meaning of *"husbands of one wife."*

2) As a textual critic, your critical interpretation of the Greek word use for one in that phrase.

I have consulted Strong on this topic and found that MIA ("one"), if that's the correct Greek word, at least to me, holds no special meaning referring to polygamy. I have found it paired with many other words not related to marriage such as one commandment, one hour, one piece, one tittle, one fold, etc.

Concerning the doctrinal interpretation, I think *"husbands of one wife"* could refer to polygamy, but should not be restricted to just that interpretation. In my mind, it could refer to divorce with equal force. But upon that argument, I feel confident that the person who disagrees with me would bring up the lawful divorce factor in 1 Corinthians.

Questions on Marriage, Re-Marriage, & Women

I apologize for the length of this e-mail, but I feel this issue bears my utmost care and attention considering that the Scriptural administration of God's House in my local assembly hangs in the balance. Any help or guidance you can give me will be greatly appreciated.

ANSWER #391

Just a few comments in writing. If you want more information, you can call me at 856-854-4747 and I can talk with you more.

1. First of all, I do not believe that a woman should be on a committee to revise a church's doctrine. This is a man's job.

2. Secondly, the word for "one" is in the feminine (MIAS) gender. HEIS is masculine, MIA is feminine and HEN is neuter. There is no special meaning for this word as the woman states.

3. *"husband(s) of one wife"* appears in three places in the New Testament: 1 Timothy 3:2; Titus 1:6 (dealing with Pastors/Bishops/Elders (one and the same office). and 1 Timothy 3:12 (dealing with deacons).

4. In BOTH of these offices, I believe the following: (1) Pastors and Deacons should be married only one time to a faithful, believing, saved, consecrated wife (unless his wife dies, and then I believe he can re-marry Scripturally since he would have only one living wife at that time thus qualifying for *"husband of one wife."*, (2) they must not be divorced or remarried for ANY reason whatsoever) and (3) they must have faithful and obedient children. This is a very strong position, but I firmly believe it is a Biblical position that I wish more people would accept and stand for.

Two Choices For Those "Departing"

QUESTION #392

You were speaking on 1 Corinthians 7:1-20. I am looking at verses 10-11 which says the wife should not depart from her husband and if she departs, she should remain unmarried. I believe that we have to stay unmarried.

ANSWER #392

If the wife walks off, she is either to (1) remain unmarried until she dies, or (2) be reconciled to her husband. This is clear from the following verses:

1 Corinthians 7:10 *"And unto the married I command, yet not I, but the Lord, Let not the wife depart from her husband*:

11 *"But and if she depart, let her remain unmarried, or be reconciled to her husband: and let not the husband put away his wife."*

Should Mates Leave One Another?

QUESTION #393

I just finished listening to Pastor Waite's sermon regarding divorce and remarriage. My question now is: Since I married a divorced woman, should I leave my marriage so she and I would no longer be called adulterers as it says in Romans 7:2-3?

ANSWER #393

Some Pastors and Bible teachers advocate breaking this kind of marriage. Since there are often children involved, that action is a difficult one to take and I would want to weigh all the facts before coming to that conclusion.

Whether you break off this marriage or whether you do not, you must both realize that God, in the consummation of this marriage, considers her to have committed adultery ("*She shall be called an adulteress*").

Matthew 5:32 says:

"*But I say unto you, That whosoever shall put away his wife, saving for the cause of fornication, causeth her to commit adultery: and whosoever shall marry her that is divorced* **committeth adultery**."

In view of this, by your marriage, you also "*committeth adultery*."

In any event, (1) both of you should repent of your actions, (2) you should ask God to forgive you for this sinful and unscriptural behavior, (3) you should teach any children that might be involved the proper meaning of marriage; (4) and you should teach any others with whom you speak that God considers it (1) a sin to divorce and remarry or (2) to marry a person who has been divorced. (3) You should henceforth teach and believe that marriage is for life as God intended it. I realize that my position on this is very rare these days and goes contrary to many Pastors and Bible teachers.

If Married To A Divorced Person

QUESTION #394

1 Corinthians 7:8-11 "*I say therefore to the unmarried and widows, It is good for them if they abide even as I. 9 But if they cannot contain, let them marry: for it is better to marry than to burn. 10 And unto the married I command, yet not I, but the Lord, Let not the wife depart from her husband: 11 But and if she depart, let her remain unmarried, or be reconciled to her husband: and let not the husband put away his wife.*"

I am married to a man who has been divorced. By doing this I realize I committed adultery. If I get a divorce from this present husband, why would you say I was to remain unmarried and sexually pure for the rest of my life? If I was never married in the sight of God and I have repented of my sin in this

Questions on Marriage, Re-Marriage, & Women

union, why would I be excluded from a Christian marriage in the future? I have no desire for this as this present union caused enough pain to last a lifetime but your reasoning confuses me.

ANSWER #394

You are now legally married in the sight of God and in the sight of man. You have a marriage license. You can only break this marriage by a divorce. To divorce your husband and marry again, you will be committing adultery once again. Do you hate your husband so much that you want a divorce from him? Where will your divorces and remarriages end? Why did you marry him in the first place if you knew he had been married before? You cannot correct your mistake by making another mistake.

1 Corinthians 7:9, printed above, is a verse for the "*unmarried and widows*" only, and not for ones like yourself who are legally married or who are adulterers. Do you not love your present husband? You say your "*present union*" is a "*pain*." Sounds to me like you are unhappy and are looking for Scripture verses to justify your leaving him. Do you have another man you want to marry all picked out? How can you think that any future marriage can be "*Christian*"? If you do not consider your present marriage to be a real marriage, what do you consider your children from this "non-marriage" to be? Do you consider them to be "*illegitimate*" and "*bastards*" therefore? If you were not really married, you had them out of wedlock. How old are these children? So they want you to leave their father? Does he want you to leave him? Does he have another wife all picked out also? This stigma upon your children will be very great indeed if you proceed in your thinking along this line. Do you want your children to bear this disgrace the rest of their lives?

> Again, stay with your present husband until death parts you and remain with your children. If you divorce him and marry again, this is double adultery in the eyes of God and of man. Think about it. There is no easy solution. You cannot turn back the clock. Again, if you leave your husband, you cannot marry again without committing adultery once again. If you have this standard, you must remain unmarried for the rest of your life.

The following verses are very clear.

1 Corinthians 7:10-11, 27 "*And unto the married I command, yet not I, but the Lord, Let not the wife depart from her husband: 11 But and if she depart, let her remain unmarried, or be reconciled to her husband: and let not the husband put away his wife. . . . 27 Art thou bound unto a wife? seek not to be loosed. Art thou loosed from a wife? seek not a wife.*"

Effects Of Divorce On Children
QUESTION #395

Proverbs 28:13 says: *"He that covereth his sins shall not prosper: but whoso confesseth and forsaketh them shall have mercy."*

My concern with your advice is the message it gives my children concerning sin (Proverbs 28:13). Am I living by faith if I remain in a situation I now know is sin? I realize sin has consequences and mine might be foregoing a marriage that isn't a true marriage at all. How can I have a relationship with a man that God calls adultery and just keep on living for Christ? My conscience wouldn't allow the relationship to continue. I'm also concerned with the scripture 1 Corinthians 5:9-11. How do I obey that?

Another concern is that I don't know what to do with the issue of obedience to my husband who disagrees with this position of no remarriage and believes his sin is under the blood. If I'm married, I must obey and if what I have is a state license to cohabit, obedience to my husband is not the issue (Acts 5:29). Also, how does one stay married to a man that she is not really married to and continue with a physical relationship trying to obey 1Corinthians 7:5?

ANSWER #395

If you and your children do not choose to remain with your husband as a wife and father, the only choice left you is to break the marriage, remain unmarried, single, sexually pure the rest of your life, and provide for yourself and your children financially by working (and/or by their working) the rest of your life as a single mother and grandmother. Is this what you want to do? Remember, it is a life-long choice of 20, 30, 50, or 60 years in length, depending on your age, which cannot be reversed.

Some Pastors hold to this view and teach it and preach it. It is a very difficult road to walk. I do not know the entire background of your situation, so my counsel cannot be complete without it.

Divorce Prior To Salvation
QUESTION #396

Is there anything in the Bible that addresses the situation where a divorced man (whose wife left him) married a single girl many years prior to his salvation? I believe we are still responsible for the sins made in ignorance but what do I do now? If I cannot go to law and my marriage was a state licensed marriage, do I just separate? My husband believes every sin is under the blood but I have had questions about my marriage since I was saved! If I'm not really married, what do I do? I have children and I don't know what to do about this mess. Can you advise?

ANSWER #396

Though different Pastors differ on this subject, I believe the Scriptures teach clearly that marriage is for life. If a person marries another person while married, this is called adultery (Mark 10:11-12; Luke 16:18; Romans 7:2-3; 1 Corinthians 7:10-11; 27).

However, when adultery has taken place and a person marries another person they must recognize it as sin, repent of it, ask God's forgiveness, teach others the truth about marriage being for life, and limit their service in the local church accordingly. Where there are children involved, it is very complicated, and in my judgment, it is better for the marriage to remain for the sake of the children and continue in a humble, repentant spirit the rest of your lives.

I know this sounds contradictory, but we cannot turn back the clock and rectify the mistakes we might have made in the past. We must go on and, if we are saved, we must live for the Lord Jesus Christ the rest of our lives.

Unmarried Sleeping In Same House?

QUESTION #397

What do you think about an unmarried female and an unmarried male sleeping under the same roof but not in the same bed. I have my strong opinion on the subject, but I wanted to get yours. Thanks for your advice!

ANSWER #397

I would certainly be opposed to such an arrangement in line with 1 Thessalonians 5:22–*"Abstain from all appearance of evil."*

Are Women Preachers Biblical?

QUESTION #398

Are women preachers Biblical? Should women teach men?

ANSWER #398

Women preachers are not Biblical. Nor is it Biblical for women to teach men, or a class with both women and men together. I am working on 1 Timothy to publish as our next *PREACHING VERSE BY VERSE* book. I just went over this theme the other day in my first draft. Here is what I have written on it.

1 Timothy 2:12

"But I suffer not a woman to teach, nor to usurp authority over the man, but to be in silence."

The word for "*suffer*" is EPITREPO. It means: "*to turn to, transfer, commit, instruct; to permit, allow, give leave.*" In other words, God does not permit or allow "*women to teach, nor to usurp authority over the man.*"

According to the Words of God, there should be no women preachers of any kind. Yet, as of 1989, here are some of the numbers of women in full-time church ministry:
    4,743 in the United Methodist churches
    4,000 in the Assemblies of God churches
    2,419 in the Presbyterian Church U.S.A. churches
    1,803 in the United Church of Christ churches
    1,358 in the Evangelical Lutheran churches
    1,225 in the Southern Baptist churches

This totals 155,480 in "*full-time church ministry.*" 84 of the 166 denominations in our country ordain women to full-time ministry. In 1989, this was 7.9% of all the U.S. clergy (National & International Religion Report, March 13, 1989)

The Scriptures are clear about women preachers. The word used for "*usurp authority*" is AUTHENTEO. It means various things: "*one who with his own hands kills another or himself; one who acts on his own authority, autocratic; an **absolute master**; to govern, **exercise dominion over** one.*" In other words, a "*woman*" is not allowed by God to "*exercise dominion*" or be an "*absolute master*" over the "*man*" (which is ARSEN or "*male*"). The Women's Liberation Movement does not go along with this verse at all.

When I was a student at Dallas Theological Seminary, I worked at a Baptist Mexican Mission for a year or so. A woman was my superior in that Mission. After a while, I had to resign because I was the pastor and it was very uncomfortable for a woman to be in authority over me in the affairs of that mission church.

The first church I pastored after my five years on active duty as a Naval Chaplain was Immanuel Baptist Church in Newton, Massachusetts. One of the most outspoken women in the congregation was the wife of a powerful deacon. It was said that she made the "snowballs," but he threw them. She was a woman out of place. I remember one particular night I was trying to turn the lights in the church off. She did not want those lights turned off so there was a battle over the light switch. It was a mess. The Lord Jesus Christ has the proper "*authority.*" There are many uses of "*authority*" in the New Testament.

    Matthew 7:29

"*For he taught them as one having **authority**, and not as the scribes.*"

    John 5:27

"*And hath given him **authority** to execute judgment also, because he is the Son of man*".

    Acts 9:14

"*And here he hath **authority** from the chief priests to bind all that call on thy name.*"

Questions on Marriage, Re-Marriage, & Women

Titus 2:15
*"These things speak, and exhort, and rebuke with all **authority**. Let no man despise thee."*

In summary, I do not believe women should teach mixed classes in Sunday School. I firmly believe that this practice is contrary to this verse. There is no Biblical prohibition for women to teach women, but men should teach men and mixed classes of men and women.

When Should Women Pray?
QUESTION #399
I would like to know if it is right for women to pray in the congregation? Also can a believer drink alcohol, work in a beer house or Motel?
ANSWER #399
1. Though they can pray in women's meetings, I do not believe women should lead in prayer in a mixed (male and female) congregation, meeting, or group. 1 Timothy 2:8 makes this clear. The word for *"men"* is ANER which refers only to males.

1 Timothy 2:8
*"I will therefore that **men** pray every where, lifting up holy hands, without wrath and doubting."*

2. I do not believe a saved person should drink alcohol or work in a beer house. I see nothing wrong with working in a proper motel, however.

Should Riplinger Teach Men?
QUESTION #400
I'm not sure I understand certain roles of women yet. For instance, a woman can write a book defending the King James Bible, which might be used by males but she isn't to teach a mixed group in a Bible study. I'm not sure I understand this yet. How would it be any different from a man using a book as an education resource written by a woman and a man deciding to come to a Bible study where a woman is teaching?

Also, I'm wondering about a woman being out front in the doctrinal wars (for instance, Gail Riplinger), where she would be in that whole debate type of thing, instead of the men answering to each other in the doctrinal war debates and being out front and the women more behind, protected, yet still working in the Word.

ANSWER #400

You have a good point here, one that others have raised as well. I guess a woman has a right to write a book, but since it is on Bible doctrine, it is somewhat of a problem because her books are used to teach men. Not only that, but she goes out in meetings and on videos which are received by many men as well. Gail Riplinger did not stop with one book (*New Age Bible Versions*) but has written many others. Her latest book (as this book is being written) is over 2,000 pages in length. It is called *Hazardous Materials*. In it, she condemns all Hebrew and Greek lexicons. This book has been answered by Dr. Kirk DiVietro and Dr. H. D. Williams in a 416-page book entitled *Cleaning-Up Hazardous Materials* (**BFT #3457 @ $25.00 +$10.00 S&H**).

After that book was completed, Gail Riplinger wrote a 61-page tirade entitled *TRAITORS* in which she called me and two other members of my family by this name, implying and stating that we (and ten others she names) are like Judas Iscariot and hence will end up in the lake of fire in Hell. I have answered his book in my 134-page book entitled: *A WARNING!! On Gail Riplinger's KJB & Multiple Inspiration HERESY.*(**BFT #3464 @ $13.00 + $7.00 S&H**).

It should be the men who write about their defense of the King James Bible, not the women. That is my Biblical opinion on this question, just the same as women should not teach mixed audiences with men. It violates clearly 1 Timothy 2:12 which says clearly: "*But I suffer not a woman to teach, nor to usurp authority over the man, but to be in silence.*" Gail Riplinger has been guilty of a very clear violation of this extremely clear Bible command! And she is unrepentant about it! On the contrary, she fights and battles with those of us who point out her violation of clear Scripture in this matter.

Index of Words and Phrases

1 Corinthians 10:31	61
1 Corinthians 16:1-2	76
1 Corinthians 16:19	71
1 Corinthians 16:2	79
1 Corinthians 5:9	84, 136
1 Corinthians 6:12	61
1 Corinthians 6:9	90
1 Corinthians 7:8-11	134
1 Corinthians 7:9	135
1 Corinthians 9:27	18, 61
1 John 1:1	27
1 John 2:15-17	61
1 John 5:16	18
1 John 5:7-8	iii, 10
1 John 5:8	11, 19
1 John, 2 John, 3 John, and Revelation	6
1 Kings 17:21-22	52
1 Kings 2:3	48
1 Peter 1:2	17, 101
1 Peter 5:1-2	104
1 Thessalonians 5:22	137
1 Timothy 1:10	90
1 Timothy 2:8	14, 139
1 Timothy 3:16	95
1 Timothy 3:5	105
1 Timothy 5:14 And "Women"	22
14 requirements that Dean Burgon needed to revise the TR	82
1598 Beza's 5th Edition Greek	23, 26, 28, 32, 92, 94, 114, 119, 126
1611 KJV	9
18 Uncials for the last 12 verses of Mark	30
1881, the date of the Westcott and Hort Greek and E.R.V.	6, 111, 124
190 passages in Beza's Appendix	32
1906 and 1912 editions of Hebrew used the Ben Chayyim text	57
1909 Spanish with some Critical Text readings	94
1948-1953, my years at Dallas Theological Seminary	104
2 Chronicles 33:19	110
2 Corinthians 12:2	31
2 Corinthians 6:14	84

2 John 7-11 78
2 Samuel 12:22-23 63
2 Timothy 2:15 23
2 Timothy 3:16--4:2 66
2 Timothy 4:2 103
2,856 Greek N.T. Words 108
2,886 words shorter 121, 122
20,000--30, 000 Footnote Suggested Changes in Kittel & Stuttgartensia .. 58
201-400 questions in this second book iii
31,101 verses in the King James Bible 66, 117
32 years ago 82
356 doctrinal and historical errors in the Gnostic Critical Greek Text 13
356 doctrinal passages 4, 60, 108, 110, 121-123
356 passages 86
5th column of Origen's HEXAPLA Bible--the Septuagint's (LXX) origin . 42
5th edition of Beza, 1598, the Greek basis for the KJB N.T. 23, 114
600 cursives favoring the last 12 verses of Mark 30
791,328 Words in the King James Bible 117
8,000 differences between the N.T. TR and CT 6, 13, 60, 108, 122
8,000 Differences Between the Critical Text and the TR 6, 60
82 years after Erasmus, 1516, was Beza's edition of 1598 92
82 years after that of Erasmus 32
85 verses per day to read the King James Bible in one year 56, 66
A Defense of 1 John 5:7-8 .... iii, 10
A man convinced against his will 7, 11
A WARNING!! On Gail Riplinger's KJB--my book 69, 88, 140
A.B., M.A., and Ph.D. 99
A.D. 90 and 100, the end of the N.T. writings 65
ab omnibus receptum "received by all" 26
Abel's Faithful Offering 41
About the Author iv
Abstain from all appearance of evil 137
ACCC (American Council of Christian Churches) 82, 83
accredited schools 98, 99
Acknowledgments .... ii, iv
Acts 12 3
Acts 13:48 And Hyper-Calvinism 29
Acts 18:18 10
Acts 2:38 14
Acts 2:46 71
Acts 20:17 .... 72, 102, 104

Index of Words and Phrases

Acts 20:17-28 104
Acts 20:20 71
Acts 28:30 71
Acts 5:29 136
Acts 5:42 71
Acts 7:45 118
adultery 130, 131, 134-137
Advisory Council of the Dean Burgon Society (DBS) 127
agree to disagree 7, 10, 11
Ahaziah 44
Albigenses 123
Albigenses, Darby, & "Hell" 123
Alcohol, total abstention .... iii, 61, 62, 139
Alexandria, Egypt 12, 13, 75
Almeida Corrigida Fiel (TBS Portuguese translation) 127
Ambassador Baptist College 99
American Bible Society 57
American Council of Christian Churches (ACCC) 82
Amos 5:24 5
Amos 5:6 52
Amos 5:7 5
Analysis Of NKJV For Laymen 127
ANALYTICAL GREEK LEXICON 45
ANALYTICAL HEBREW LEXICON 45
ANER ("male") 14, 139
Annotated Greek New Testament 32, 119
Any Faithful Modern Translations? 125
aorist Greek tense 45, 119
apograph (copy) 46
Arabic translation 59
Aramaic ... 4, 9, 24, 25, 32, 34, 40, 42, 46, 55, 56, 68, 69, 79, 80, 83, 100, 108, 115-122, 125-127
Are There Errors In The KJB? 119
Are Translations "Inspired" by God? 79
ARMINIAN VIEW 74
articles 24, 51, 55, 95, 101
ASV of 1901 124
Authorship of John's Gospel 6
Autographs And Apographs 46
babies 63
baptism 15, 64, 100

Baptism of the Spirit occurs upon salvation 64
Baptist Bride view is erroneous 83
Baptist churches 70, 71, 83, 104, 111, 138
Baptist school 98
baptized by the Holy Spirit into one body 64
Barbara Egan, our BFT Secretary ii
behemoth and a leviathan 53
Berry, George Ricker, his interlinear Greek N.T. 28
Beza, edition used for KJB 23, 26, 28, 32, 92, 94, 114, 119, 126
Beza's 5th Edition (1598) Is Superior 32
Beza's 5th edition, 1598 .... 28, 119
BFT #1139 ....4, 30
BFT #1442 ....4, 108, 126, 127
BFT #1594 ....110, 115, 122
BFT #1670 ....32, 119
BFT #2185 ....95, 97
BFT #2928/P 107
BFT #2956 86
BFT #3084 ....6, 13, 60
BFT #3230 ....4, 24, 60, 86, 110
BFT #3309 iii
BFT #3464 ....69, 88, 140
BFT #611 82
BFT #804 ....6, 82
BFT #83 123
BFT Phone: 856-854-4452 i
Bible Against Homosexuality and Bestiality 90
Bible College 98
Bible condemns homosexuality and lesbianism 90
Bible For Today .... i-iii, 44, 45, 66, 70, 79, 83, 101, 125
Bible For Today Baptist Church .... i-iii, 66, 70, 125
Bible For Today Press i
Bible Interpretation Methods 67
Bible Preservation 8, 34, 68, 83
Bible reading 56, 66
BIBLIA HEBRAICA 57, 58
Biblical Preservation And Writers 68
bishop 62, 70-72, 104, 105
bishops 71, 72, 103-105, 133
BJU, Bob Jones University 83, 107, 124, 125
black 81

Index of Words and Phrases

Blasphemy Against the Holy Spirit 31
blood .... iii, 11, 17-19, 52, 90, 95-98, 100, 136
Bob Jones University 83
Body .... ii, 17, 18, 53, 54, 61, 64, 66, 67, 72, 73, 83, 89, 102
Bonaventure and Abraham Elzevir 26
Bouw, Dr. Gerardus D. (author of *The Book of Bible Problems*) 44
Brazil 127
Bride 83
British and Foreign Bible Society 57
BROWN BOX of www.BibleForToday.org website 67, 125
Bruce Metzger, Gnostic Critical Text defender 6, 22
Burgon, Dean John William ii-6, 16, 30, 79, 81, 82, 112, 127
Burgon's Position On The T.R. 81
Burgon's Warnings on Revision 6, 82
buried in a Protestant cemetery (Roman Catholic Erasmus) 92
Byzantine Text 60
Calvinism .... iii, 29, 69, 73, 91, 100, 101
Calvinism & The Decrees Of God 73
CambOxfDifferences.102.pdf (Cambridge & Oxford differences) 110
Cambridge Press King James Bibles 13, 14, 107-110, 116, 119
Cambridge 1769 Text 107
Cambridge/Oxford KJB Differences 109
Camping, Harold 99
Can 1769 KJB Be Called KJB? 107
Cardinal Ximenes, compiler of the Complutensian Polyglot 23
Cardinal's hat, refused by Erasmus 92
CASE FOR THE KING JAMES BIBLE 123
Cathari sect in the early church 123
Catholic versions 92
Catholic, Protestant, Jewish, Islamic, Buddhist 63
Catholics 91, 92
CCM (Contemporary Christian Music) 10
Cephas 9, 24, 25
Changes In N.T. Name Spellings 116
Chapter And Verse Divisions, made by whom and when 115, 116
Charismatics 65
Christ Abolished Moses' Law .... iii, 14
Christ In The Old Testament 50, 51
Christmas 68, 73, 100
Christophany 58
Christ's blood 95

Christ's Body 102
Christ's chosen Body 17
church . i-4, 10, 11, 14, 15, 17, 18, 22, 24, 30, 33, 34, 60, 64, 66, 67, 69-72,
        75, 77, 79, 83, 84, 86, 89, 91, 92, 94, 99-105, 110, 112, 113, 120,
                                            123-125, 127, 132, 137, 138
church began 33, 34
Church Phone: 856-854-4747 i
Churches And Elders? 104
Classical Greek 12
Cloud, David W. 69, 71, 92
cognate languages to Hebrew 40
Col. Jose Pedro Almeida from Brazil 127
Colas, Ralph 82, 83
Collingswood, New Jersey i
Colossians 4:15 71
Comfort, Ray (and also the noun) 16, 45, 94, 118, 138
committing adultery 135
Complutensian Polyglot by Cardinal Ximenes 23, 113
Contemporary Evangelicalism 82
Conversions And Modern Versions 108
conversions to Christ 108
corporate election 102
Critical Text begun by the Gnostics of Egypt 3, 6, 24, 60, 83
Critical Text camp 6
Dallas Theological Seminary 24, 42, 44, 104, 138
Dan Wallace, teacher at Dallas Theological Seminary .... iii, 24
Dana and Mantey, authors of *Intermediate Greek Grammar* 13
Daniel 9:11 49
Daniel Bomberg edition of 1524-1525, basis of the KJB's O.T. 57
Daniel S. Waite, assistant to Pastor D. A. Waite ii
Darby, John Nelson, editor of a Bible translation 59, 121-124
Darby's French Bible 123
Darby's Translation, follows the Gnostic text many places 59
David Cloud 69, 71, 92
Deacon 70, 129, 132, 138
deacons 62, 70, 72, 104, 129, 132, 133
Dead Sea Scrolls 55, 56
Dean Burgon, John William .... ii, iii, 5, 6, 16, 30, 79, 81, 82, 112, 127
Dean Burgon Society .... ii, 5, 79, 81, 82
Dean John W. Burgon 4
death of the mate 130

Index of Words and Phrases

Debating BJU Pastors On TR 124
Decrees of God .... iii, 73
Defending the King James Bible 23, 110, 111, 115, 122, 139
Defined King James Bible ...... iv, 3, 13, 27, 92, 109, 116, 117, 119, 126
Defined King James Bible Order Form iv
degrees 87, 88, 99
degrees of blessings in Heaven 87
degrees of punishment in Hell 87, 88
derived inspiration not correct iii
Deuteronomy 32:43 58
Did Jesus Christ and the Apostles Quote From the LXX 42
Differences In Various KJB Bibles 108
Differences Of "Soul" & "Spirit" 52
disqualified to be a pastor 104
Distortions on Bible Versions 107
Divietro, Dr. Kirk 42, 76, 92, 140
divorce .... iii, iv, 129-132, 134-136
Divorce Prior To Salvation 136
DKJB (*Defined King James Bible*) 9
doctrinal importance 60
dominant Graeco-Syrian Text of A.D. 359, the Traditional Text 82
Don't Trust The Dead Sea Scrolls 55
Doxology 33
Dr Ralph Colas 82
Dr Richard Harris 82
Dr Rolland McCune 82
Dr. and Mrs. H. D. Williams ii
Dr. Anderson 57
Dr. D. A. Waite 1, 1, 46
Dr. DiVietro 42
Dr. Frederick Scrivener 26
Dr. Gerardus D. Bouw 44
Dr. Humberto Gomez 93, 94
Dr. Jack Moorman 6, 24, 60, 95
Dr. Kirk Divietro 92, 140
Dr. McIntire 83
Dr. Merrill F. Unger 44
Dr. Moorman 10-12, 24
Dr. S. H. Tow 109
Dr. Thomas Strouse 51
Dr. Unger 44

drinking .... iii, 18, 61, 62
Drinking Alcohol .... iii, 61
DTS (Dallas Theological Seminary) 99
Early Manuscripts, Church Fathers 4, 24, 60, 110
Easter 3, 4, 100
Effects Of Divorce On Children 136
Egan, Barbara .... ii, 1, 6, 33, 34, 57, 83, 89, 94
EKKLESIA 72
elder 70, 71, 77, 102, 104, 120
Elders are required 70
Elect 73, 74, 101, 102
election .... iii, 100-102
Election & Hyper-Calvinism 101
Elias 109, 116
Elias vs. Elijah 109
Elzevir edition of the Greek N.T. 26, 114
Ephesians 2:1 14
Ephesians 2:8 .... iii, 32, 76, 101
Ephesians 2:8-9 Explained Clearly .... iii, 32
Ephesians 5:11 84
Erasmus 23, 32, 92, 113
Erasmus And The KJB 92
Erasmus in 1516 .... 23, 32
Erasmus' edition of 1516 92
errors .... iii, 13, 22, 24, 75, 76, 83, 86, 88, 94, 97, 102, 119, 121, 122, 127
Errors of Baptist "Bride" & "Body" 83
ERV of 1881 124
Esaias as Isaiah 116
ETH in Hebrew, sign of the direct object 37, 46, 50
every known Lectionary of the East backs Mark 16:9-20 30
Eve's Creation From Adam's Rib 41
Evidence Bible 118
Expository Preaching In Churches 103
EXTREME LIMITED ATONEMENT 73
Ezekiel 13:18 45
e-mail: BFT@BibleForToday.org i
false doctrines 4, 78, 104
FALSE TEXT 57
Fasting In This Dispensation 79
fax: 856-854-2464 i
feminine 9, 22, 32, 45, 76, 85, 133

Index of Words and Phrases

figure of speech 95
Filling of the Holy Spirit 64
for the remission of sins 14, 15
FOREWORD .... iii, iv
fornication 130, 131, 134
French translation 119
fundamentalism 82, 107
Fundamentalism and the Word of God 107
Fundamentalist Distortions on Bible Versions 107
Gail Riplinger 69, 80, 139, 140
Galatians 2:11-12 10
GARBC (General Association of Regular Baptist Churches) 11
GEHENNA, Greek word for Hell, the Lake of Fire 123
Genesis 1:1 .... 43, 46, 54
Genesis 19:5 91
Genesis 2:21 41
Genesis 20:16 43
Genesis 4:4 41
George Ricker Berry, editor of the Interlinear Greek N.T. 28
Germans 47
Ghost 14, 15, 18, 31, 33, 67
given by inspiration of God, refers only to originals 80, 115, 120
Giving And Tithing In The N.T. 79
Gnostic 12, 13, 22, 27, 60, 75, 83, 86, 122-124
Gnostic Critical Greek Text 22, 27, 60, 83, 86, 122-124
Gnostic Vatican Manuscript 12
God has kept His Words intact 34, 68
God has preserved His Words 125
God the Holy Spirit 10, 17, 19, 33, 34, 67, 68, 89, 120
God-breathed 80, 115
God's Gift And Christmas Gifts 68
Going To Hell For Not Using KJB? 116
Going To "Accredited" Schools 98
Gomez, Dr. Humberto, editor of Spanish Bible (RVG) 93, 94
Gospel of John 6, 25, 119
Graf and Wellhausen, German apostates 47
grammar 19, 32, 39, 46, 119
grammatical-historical 67
Greek . 4-6, 9, 10, 12-17, 19, 21-24, 26-29, 32-35, 37, 42-46, 53, 55, 59, 60,
62, 68, 69, 72, 75, 76, 79, 80, 82, 83, 85, 86, 92-94, 99, 100, 103,
108, 109, 111, 113-127, 129, 132, 140

Greek & Hebrew Tenses 45
Greek Scrivener Edition 28
Greek Septuagint (LXX) 42
Green, Jay 28
Greene, Evangelist Oliver B. 132
Griesbach, editor of a Gnostic Critical Greek Text 82, 122
groanings 17
H.A. Ironside 132
HADES 123
hapax legomenon, something used only one time 40
Harold Camping 99
Harris, Richard 82, 83
Head of the church 34
heaven 18, 30, 31, 38, 46, 54, 55, 63, 73, 83, 86, 87, 89, 100, 110, 117
Heaven or Hell 117
Hebrew   iii-4, 9, 13, 19, 20, 24, 28, 32, 34, 35, 37-46, 51-59, 68, 69, 76, 79,
                80, 83, 99, 100, 103, 108-110, 114-122, 125-127, 140
Hebrew & Greek Lexicons 44
Hebrew lexicon 40, 45, 46
Hebrew tenses 45
Hebrew Versus Septuagint (LXX) 58
Hebrew Vowel Points, present from the beginning of the Bible 51
Hebrew, Aramaic, or Greek Words 4, 34, 68, 119
Hebrews 9, 16, 18, 58, 104, 116
Hebrews 13:17 104
Hebrews 6:4 Refers To Christians 18
Hebrews 6:4-8 Explained 16
Hell 47, 63, 87-89, 100, 116, 117, 123, 130, 140
Henry, Matthew 132
heresies 80, 88, 98
heresy on the Blood of Christ 95, 97
Holy "Ghost" Or Holy "Spirit"? 33
homosexuality 89-91
house churches .... iii, 69-72
house fellowship 70
How Far Should Separation Go? 84
How To Handle Certain Critics 75
How To Handle Disagreements 74
How To "Obey" Those Who "Rule" 104
HYPER CALVINISTS 73, 74
hyper-Calvinist 69

Index of Words and Phrases

hyper-Calvinism .... iii, 29, 101
HYPER-HYPER CALVINISTS 73
I Believe In The Precious Blood, by John MacArthur, blood=death 95
I Corinthians 12:1-10. 65
I Corinthians 12:13 64
I Corinthians 12:25 64
If Bad, Why Is "Negro" Still Used? 81
illegitimately pregnant 104
imperfect 39, 45, 119
in the day of judgment 87
In The N.T., "Jesus" Or "Joshua" 118
Incarnation of God the Son 68
Index of Words and Phrases .... iv, 1, 141
indwelling 64, 67
INFRALAPSARIAN VIEW 74
inspired of God, only proper for Hebrew, Aramaic, and Greek 80, 116
Interlinear Greek-English New Testaments 28
Intermediate Grammar 19
Interpretation of Isaiah 55:11-13 39
Introductory Considerations .... iv, 1
Ireland 46, 112
Ironside, Dr.Harry 99, 132
Isaiah 55:11-13 39
ISBE, *International Standard Bible Encyclopedia* 44
ISBN #1-56848-070-9 i
itself 10, 12, 17, 39, 53, 55, 91, 114, 127
J, E, P. and D, a false view of the O.T. Hebrew documents 47
James 5:16 .... 3, 22
James 5:16 And Bruce Metzger 22
Jay P. Green 28
Jehovah's Witnesses Cult 78
Jehovah's Witnesses Material 78
Jeremiah 109, 116
Jeremiah 34:16 109
Jeremiah's "Lost" Words & the KJB 38
Jeremy for Jeremiah 116
John 1:12 111
John 12:40 25
John 14:17 33
John 17:15 84
John 20:20-22 33

John 3:13 86
John 3:16 .... 85, 102, 123
John 5:47 95
John 5:7-8 95
John 6:47 123
John MacArthur & Christ's Blood 95
John MacArthur's Heresy On The Blood 95
John Nelson Darby 121
John the Baptist 33, 34
Jones, Dr. Floyd or Bob Jones or BJU 76, 83, 96, 123
Joshua 48, 116
Joshua 1:7 48
Joshua 8:32 48
jotaetil@hotmail.com, E-mail of Col. Jose Pedro Almeida 127
Judges 19:22 91
Judgment seat of Christ 16
Kelly, William 121, 122
Kenneth Wuest 132
Kittel, Rudolf 57
KJB   iii, iv, 3-5, 10, 13, 22-24, 27, 28, 32, 35, 38, 40, 44, 45, 51, 55, 56, 58-
      60, 69, 75, 82, 83, 85, 88, 92-94, 98-100, 107-111, 115-120, 122-
      127, 140
KJB translators 4, 32, 40, 51, 118
KJB--Imperfect Tense As Aorist? 119
KJV ... 3, 4, 9, 21, 24, 40, 54, 62, 90, 91, 93, 107-110, 116, 117, 123, 124,
      126
Lamb of God 47
LAPSARIAN, referring to the fall of man 73, 74
Latin manuscripts 10
law of Moses 14, 48-50
Leading In Prayer With Unsaved 86
Lesbianism 89, 90
Lesbianism & Homosexuality 89
lesser details 82
Let them alone 7, 11, 25, 56, 74
Letteris text of 1866, similar to the Hebrew of Ben Chayyim 57
leviathan 53
Leviticus 18:23 90
Leviticus 19:18 35
Leviticus 20:13 90
LIMITED ATONEMENT 73, 74, 100

Index of Words and Phrases

local church	66, 104, 137
Lord's Supper	127
Luke 21:24	88
Luke 24:44	50
Luke 4:4	8
Luke 8:55	52, 53
Luther, Martin	23, 138
LXX, Septuagint	42, 58
LXX appeared in the 200's A.D. in Origin's day	58
MacArthur, John	iii, 95-98, 132
MacArthur's heresy on the Blood of Christ	95
Making Offerings Public	75
Malachi chapter3:8	79
Males Praying In Mixed Meetings	14
Mark 10:27	27
Mark 13:25	30
Mark 13:8	30
Mark 15:2	30
Mark 16:9-20–Right Or Wrong?	29
Mark 3:28 And John 1:42	24
Mark 6:11	87
Mark 7:10	49
mark of the beast	63
Martin Luther	23
Masoretic Text of Hebrew	44, 51, 54, 57, 58
Matt. 16:18	123
Matthew 10:14-15	87
Matthew 11:23-24	87
Matthew 12:32	31
Matthew 15:12-14	7
Matthew 16:18	9, 25, 33, 89
Matthew 16:18.	9
Matthew 18:10	63
Matthew 18:17	33
Matthew 19:1-9	49
Matthew 19:19	35
Matthew 19:26	92
Matthew 2:17	13, 116
Matthew 2:8	73
Matthew 24:36	16
Matthew 28:19-20	67

Matthew 4:4	8
Matthew 5:17	14
Matthew 5:32	134
Matthew 6:3	75
Matthew Henry	132
McCune, Rolland	82, 83
McIntire, Dr. Carl	83
Meaning Of "Grace For Grace"	19
Meaning of "Seek The Lord"	52
Meaning of "Well Pleased"	21
meanings	5, 9, 15, 25, 27, 35, 43, 45, 52, 67, 72, 99, 103, 119
Messiah	26, 47, 51
metonym for "death", John MacArthur says "blood" is	95
Metzger, Bruce	6, 22
minor changes	6, 107
Miscellaneous Questions	iii, iv
Missing in Modern Bibles: Is the Full Story Told?	12
Modern Bibles' Failings	12
Modern Versions & Salvation	120
Moorman, Dr. Jack	6, 10-12, 24, 60, 76, 86, 95
Mrs. Waite, Yvonne S.	69, 113
N.T. Elders And House Churches	70
N.T. "Judgment" And "Justice"	5
NA .	3, 6, 9, 12-16, 19, 20, 25, 26, 28, 30, 31, 37, 39, 40, 44, 45, 50, 51, 53-55, 58, 59, 62, 64, 67, 69, 71, 72, 76, 77, 80, 81, 87, 90, 91, 94, 99, 101, 109-111, 113, 115, 116, 121, 124-127, 130, 138, 140
NABV	69
Nahum 3:16	110
NASB	55
NASV	19, 40, 55, 59, 115, 124, 125
NASV, RSV, and the NRSV	19
Need A Sound Arabic Translation	59
Negro, still used today in many contexts	81
neighbour	35
neo-evangelical schools	82
NEPHALIOS, free from alcohol	62
NEPHO, free from alcohol	62
Nestle, Eberhard, of the NA or Nestle/Aland Gnostic Critical N.T.	6, 60
Nestle 27, Nestle-Aland 27th edition of the Gnostic Critical Greek N.T.	6
Nestle-Aland	6
never lead critical students of Scripture seriously astray, the TR	82

Index of Words and Phrases

New Age Bible Versions by Gail Riplinger, loaded with errors .. 69, 88, 140
New RSV 43
New Versions "Another Gospel"? 123
Newtownards in Northern Ireland 46
NIV perversion 121
NIV, NASV, RSV, NRSV, NKJV, ESV 115
NIV's 356 Doctrinal Passage Errors 86
NKJV, New King James Version 3, 40, 59, 108, 115, 124-127
Northern Ireland 46
NRSV, New Revised Standard Version 19, 115, 125
Number Of Words & Verses In KJB 117
numbers 48, 49, 67, 75, 76, 80, 99, 138
Numbers Seven & Three 67
O.T. Meaning Of "Judgment" 37
Offerings 49, 62, 75
Old Testament Quotes In The N.T. 34
Oliver Greene, evangelist 132
Omnipresence 86
ordained 29
Order Blank Pages iv
Orders: 1-800-John 10:9 i
Origin Of The Hebrew Vowel Points 51
Oxford Press King James Bibles 13, 108-110, 119
Paradise 47
passover 3, 4
Pastor D. A. Waite .... i, iii, 38, 44, 71, 73, 90
Pastor Zeller, George 94, 95
Pastoral authority 105
pastors/bishops/elders 71, 72, 103, 105, 133
Paul's Vow & Shaving His Head 10
Pentateuch .... iii, 47-50
Pentecost 33, 34, 65, 89, 91, 102
Pentecostals 65
Perverted Modern Bible Versions 110
Peter 3, 9, 10, 14, 17, 38, 51, 62, 72, 77, 80, 88, 89, 101, 103, 104
Peter Ruckman 80, 88
Ph.D. .... i, iii, 71, 73, 90, 98, 99
Philemon 2 71
Philippians 4:13 95
Pilate 30, 31, 80
pleased 21, 46

Plymouth Brethren 122, 124
POD, Print On Demand, with Dr. H. D. Williams ii
polygamy 132
Pope 91, 92
Pope of Rome 91
Portuguese Bible 127
possible .... ii, iii, 27, 58, 67, 68, 92, 108, 119, 126
Preach the Word 103
predestination 101
Princeton 22
probable 126
prospered 76, 79
Protestant cemetery, Erasmus buried in 92
Proverbs 21:1 42
Proverbs 18:24 59
Proverbs 22:10 7
Proverbs 23:31 61
Proverbs 28:13 136
Proverbs 29:9 11
Psalm 106:15 55
Psalm 119's Hebrew Letters 37
Psalm 23:5 38
Pulpit Attacks & Gail Riplinger 69
questions answered .... 1, iii, 1
Questions On Matthew 24:36 16
Questions on the KJB & Various Bible Versions iv
Questions on the N.T. & Its Texts iv
Questions on the O.T. & Hebrew Subjects iv
quick-prayerism 66
Radio and Audio Film Commission 83
Rapture of the born-again Christians 88, 89, 100
Ray Comfort 118
recognize it as sin 137
Reese Chronological Bible 34
Reformed theology 29
regeneration 64
Reina Valera Version 1960, filled with many Gnostic Critical readings ... 94
remain unmarried 131, 133-136
Remarriage .... iii, iv, 129, 130, 132, 134, 136
remission of sins 14, 15
reproving of sin 64

Index of Words and Phrases

requires Revision, Dean Burgon said of the KJB in minor places 82
restraining sin, a ministry of God the Holy Spirit 64
revision 5, 6, 81, 82, 88, 132
Revision Revised 5, 82, 88
Riplinger, Gail Ludwig Latessa Kaleda Riplinger 69, 80, 88, 139, 140
Robertson, A. T. 13
Roman Catholic 22, 91, 92, 113, 114
Roman Catholic Church 91, 92
Roman Catholic Confessional 22
Roman Catholics 91, 92
Romanian 13
Romans 1 And God's Words 20
Romans 1:16 94
Romans 1:26 90
Romans 1:27 90
Romans 12:1-2 61
Romans 2:8 12
Romans 5:21 19
Romans 7:2-3 .... 130, 131, 134, 137
Romans 8:16 and 8:26 .... 10, 28
Romans 8:27 17
Romans 8:29-30 101
RSV, Revised Standard Version 19, 43, 115, 124, 125
Ruckman, Peter 80, 88
Ruckman/Riplinger KJB Heresies 88
Rudolf Kittel, editor of Biblia Hebraica with the Ben Asher Hebrew 57
RVG, Reina Valera Gomez, a good Spanish edited by Dr. Golmez ... 93, 94
safe 27, 63
Salvation For The Pope & Catholics 91
same sex unions 89
Sarah--"Scolded" Or "Reproved"? 43
schools 42, 82, 98, 99
Scofield, C. I. 27, 132
scolded Peter, Paul did 10
scribes and Pharisees 7
Scrivener, Dr. Frederick, editor of TR Greek 26, 28, 32, 59, 60, 112
sealing 64
Second 200 Questions Answered .... iii, 1
secular school 99
seminary 24, 42, 44, 73, 98, 99, 104, 138
separated church 66

Separation And Prayer Requests 85
Septuagint (LXX) 42, 58, 76
Seven Hills & Mark Of The Beast 63
She shall be called an adulteress 131, 134
Sheol, Old Testament Hades or place of departed spirits 47, 54, 55
Shintoist, Taoist, Christian Science, Jehovah Witnesses 63
Should Mates Leave One Another? 134
Should New Versions Be Trusted? 125
Should Riplinger Teach Men? 139
Sinai manuscript (Aleph), a false Greek text 4, 6, 13, 30, 75, 112, 122
soul 12, 52, 53, 55, 66, 67, 77, 130
soul-winning 66, 67
sovereign 42
Spanish Bible 93, 94
Spanish, French, Latin, Greek, Hebrew 76
speculation 68, 99
spirit . 8, 10, 11, 15, 17-19, 28, 31, 33-35, 53, 64, 67, 68, 89, 109, 120, 137
Stephanus, editor of a Traditional Geek Text 28, 93, 114
Stephens 1550 Greek text 28
Stephens Greek New Testament 9
STREAMING VIDEOS 125
Strouse, Dr. Thomas 51
Stuttgartensia, an edition of *BIBLIA HEBRAICA* (Hebrew Bible) 57, 58
SUBLAPSARIAN VIEW 74
SUPRALAPSARIAN VIEW 73
Systematic Theology 73
Table of Contents iv
TASSO 29
TBS, Trinitarian Bible Society 28, 127
ten early translations 30
tenses 21, 45
Textum ergo habes, a "text" which has (been received by all) 26
Textus Receptus 5, 6, 22, 26, 59, 60, 82, 93, 94, 111, 123, 125, 126
Th.D. .... i, iii, 71, 73, 90, 98, 99
Th.M. and Th.D. from Dallas Seminary, I received 99
That which 28, 33, 65, 90, 91, 112
The ACCC And The Bible Issues 82
The Authenticity Of Mark 16:9-20 .... iii, 4
The Author Of The Pentateuch .... iii, 47
THE BOOK OF BIBLE PROBLEMS, by Dr. Gerardus Bouw 44
The Competing N.T. Greek Texts 59

Index of Words and Phrases

The Darby And Kelly Translations 121
The Date Of The "Textus Receptus" 26
The Evidence Bible 118
The Freedom of Man's Will 42
The Holy Spirit Before Pentecost 33
The Holy Spirit's Ministries 64
The KJB & "Derived Inspiration" 115
The Last Twelve Verses of Mark by Dean John William Burgun 4, 30
The Meaning of Acts 2:38 14
The Meaning Of Number "Ten" 99
The Meaning of PROS AUTON 13
The Meaning Of "Might" 19
The Meaning of "Written By" 9
The New King James Version Analyzed 127
The Old Testament In Greek (LXX) 42
The Omnipresence of Jesus Christ 86
The Proof of the Pudding Is In The Eating 99
The Received Versus Critical Text 6
The Recommended Hebrew Text 57
The RVG & Spanish Bible Issues 93, 94
The Sevenfold Spirit of God 8
The Teachings of Psalm 23:5 38
THE TWO HEBREW TEXTS 57
The Use of ETH In Hebrew 46
The Work of God Holy Spirit 17
Theophany 58
THEOPNEUSTOS, "God-breathed" 115, 120
THREE DIFFERENCES between the Cambridge and Oxford KJB's ... 109
Titus 1:5 .... 70, 105
tongues 7, 65
Tongues And Other Spiritual Gifts 65
Torah, the first five books of the O.T. 44
Tow, Dr. S. H. Or Dr. Timothy 21, 25, 90, 94, 109
TR ... iii, 3-6, 9, 10, 13, 15, 16, 20-25, 27-30, 32, 34, 35, 38-40, 42-44, 46,
    48, 51, 54, 55, 57, 59-61, 66-68, 75, 78-82, 85, 86, 93, 94, 99, 100,
    104, 108, 111, 114-127, 137, 140
Traditional Hebrew Masoretic Text 44, 54
Traditional Texts 125
translation errors 119
Translation Of Verses In Mark 30
translators 4, 10, 32, 40, 42, 51, 54, 59, 118, 119, 126

Tregelles, Samuel, a Plymouth Brethren man, but for the CT 122, 124
Trinitarian Bible Society (TBS) 57, 127
Trinity 11, 33, 39
TRUE TEXT 57
true, reliable, and accurate, the King James Bible 115
Two Choices For Those "Departing" 133
Two Versions On Genesis 27:39-40 55
UBS, United Bible Societies 6
unaccredited 98, 99
Understanding Proverbs 18:24 59
Unger, Dr. Merrill F. 44
United Bible Societies (UBS) 6
United Negro College Fund, still uses "Negro" in its title 81
unleavened bread 3, 4
UNLIMITED ATONEMENT 74
Unmarried Sleeping In Same House? 137
Vatican Manuscript "B" a Gnostic Critical Text 4, 6, 12, 13, 30, 75, 112, 122
Vatican ("B") and Sinai (Aleph) manuscripts, two corrupt MSS 4
Vatican and Sinai MSS, two corrupt manuscripts 4, 6
Verses Against Drinking Alcohol .... iii, 61
Vision Forum, a reformed theology group 69
Vowel Points, began from the beginning of Genesis 51
Waite, Dr. D. A.++ 1, i-iii, 1, 38, 44, 46, 69, 71, 73, 78, 90, 96-98, 113, 126
Wallace, Dan .... iii, 24
Warren, Rick 104
water baskets 15, 64
water baptism and baptism of the Spirit 64
Website: www.BibleForToday.org i
Westcott/Hort, founders of the false Gnostic Critical Greek text in 1881 ... 6
What About The Portuguese Bible? 127
What Does Word-Gender Mean? 76
What Does "Even" Mean? 111
What Is A Church Elder? 102
What Is A "Leviathan"? 53
What Is A "Neighbour"? 35
What Is A "Separated" Church? 66
What Is The TORAH? 44
What Is "Sheol"? 54
What Is "Vision Forum"? 69
What TR Before Beza's 5th in 1598? 23
What's Wrong With The NKJV? 108

Index of Words and Phrases

When Should Women Pray? 139
Where Is "Paradise" Now? 47
which . 3-14, 17, 19-22, 25-30, 32, 33, 35, 38-41, 46, 48, 50, 51, 54-56, 58, 61, 63, 65, 66, 69-71, 73-75, 77, 78, 80, 82, 83, 85-87, 89-91, 93, 94, 98-100, 102, 107-109, 111-117, 119-126, 129-133, 136, 138-140
Which Greek Interlinear N.T.? 28
which is in heaven 63, 86
Who Was Melchisedec? 58
whosoever believeth 102
Why Are There Various Wordings? 8
Why Not Use Modern Versions? 122
Why Sunday, Easter, & Christmas? 100
Why The "Spirit Itself"? 10
Why "Jeremy" Not "Jeremiah" 13
Why "Which" In 1 John 1:1? 27
Will Babies Go To Heaven? 63
William Jones 123
Wise Men And Christmas Gifts 73
word-gender 76
worship 52, 58, 72, 79, 101, 117
Would Dean Burgon Revise The TR? .... iii, 5
written by 139
www.BibleForToday.org .... i, 14, 56, 66, 76, 95, 126
Ximenes, Cardinal, editor of the Complutensian Polyglot 23, 113
Yearly Bible Reading Schedule, 85 verse per day 66
Yearly Bible Reading–How? 56
young child 73
Yvonne Sanborn Waite, wife of Dr. D. A. Waite ii
Zeller, Pastor George 94, 95
"Cephas," "Peter," And "Rock" 9
"Corporate Election" Explained 17
"Easter" Or "Passover"? 3
"Faults" And "Sins" 3
"Heaven" Or "Heavens"? 54
"Indignation" and "Wrath" 12
"Neighbour" Or "Others" 111
"Pillows To All Amholes" 45
"Rock" As A Name For "God" 51
"Should Not" In John 12:40 25
"Spirit" Or "spirit"? 19

"Study Bible" Recommendation 27
"Study" In 2 Timothy 2:15 23
"Temptation" Versus "Trial" 25
"With" In Mark 10:27 27
"Worship" Of The KJB?--A Smear 117

About the Author

The author of this book, Dr. D. A. Waite, received a B.A. (Bachelor of Arts) in classical Greek and Latin from the University of Michigan in 1948, a Th.M. (Master of Theology), with high honors, in New Testament Greek Literature and Exegesis from Dallas Theological Seminary in 1952, an M.A. (Master of Arts) in Speech from Southern Methodist University in 1953, a Th.D. (Doctor of Theology), with honors, in Bible Exposition from Dallas Theological Seminary in 1955, and a Ph.D. in Speech from Purdue University in 1961. He holds both New Jersey and Pennsylvania teacher certificates in Greek and Language Arts.

He has been a teacher in the areas of Greek, Hebrew, Bible, Speech, and English for over thirty-five years in ten schools, including one junior high, one senior high, four Bible institutes, two colleges, two universities, and one seminary. He served his country as a Navy Chaplain for five years on active duty; pastored three churches; was Chairman and Director of the Radio and Audio-Film Commission of the American Council of Christian Churches; since 1969, has been Founder, President, and Director of THE BIBLE FOR TODAY; since 1978, has been President of the DEAN BURGON SOCIETY; has produced over 800 other studies, books, audio cassettes, CD's, VCR's, or DVD's on various topics; and is heard on a thirty-minute weekly program, IN DEFENSE OF TRADITIONAL BIBLE TEXTS, on radio, and streaming on the Internet at BibleForToday.org, 24/7/365.

Dr. and Mrs. Waite have been married since 1948; they have four sons, one daughter, and, at present, eight grandchildren, and nine great-grandchildren. Since October 4, 1998, he has been the Pastor of the Bible For Today Baptist Church in Collingswood, New Jersey.

Order Blank (p. 1)

Name:_____

Address:_____

City & State:_____Zip:_____

Credit Card #:_____Expires:_____

Latest Books

[ ] Send The Second 200 Questions Answered By Dr. D. A. Waite (176 pp. perfect bound ($12.00 + $5.00 S&H)
[ ] Send *The First 200 Questions Answered By Dr. D. A. Waite* (184 pp. perfect bound (12.00 + $5.00 S&H)
[ ] Send *A Warning on Gail Riplinger's KJB & Multiple Inspiration HERESY* By Pastor D. A. Waite, 137 pp. ($11+$7 S&H)
[ ] Send *A Critical Answer to James Price's King James Only-ism* By Pastor D. A. Waite, 184pp, perfect bound ($11+$5 S&H)
[ ] Send *The KJB's Superior Hebrew & Greek Words* by Pastor D. A. Waite, 104 pp., perfect bound ($10+$5 S&H)
[ ] Send *Soulwinning's Versions-Perversions* by Pastor D. A. Waite, booklet, 28 pp. ($6+$3 S&H) fully indexed
[ ] Send *2 Timothy--Preaching Verse by Verse*, by Pastor D. A. Waite, 250 pages, perfect bound ($11+$5 S&H) fully indexed.
[ ] Send *A Critical Answer to God's Word Preserved* by Pastor D. A. Waite, 192 pp. perfect bound ($11.00+$5.00 S&H)

The Most Recently Published Books

[ ] Send *8,000 Differences Between Textus Receptus & Critical Text* by Dr. J. A. Moorman, 544 pp., hrd. back ($20+$5 S&H)
[ ] *Early Manuscripts, Church Fathers, & the Authorized Version* by Dr. Jack Moorman, $20+$5 S&H. Hardback
[ ] Send *The LIE That Changed the Modern World* by Dr. H. D. Williams ($16+$5 S&H) Hardback book
[ ] Send *With Tears in My Heart* by Gertrude G. Sanborn. Hardback 414 pp. ($25+$5 S&H) 400 Christian Poems

Send or Call Orders to:
THE BIBLE FOR TODAY
900 Park Ave., Collingswood, NJ 08108
Phone: 856-854-4452; FAX:--2464; Orders: 1-800 JOHN 10:9
E-Mail Orders: BFT@BibleForToday.org; Credit Cards OK

Order Blank (p. 2)

Name:_____

Address:_____

City & State:_____ Zip:_____

Credit Card #:_____ Expires:_____

Preaching Verse by Verse Books

[ ] Send *2 Timothy--Preaching Verse by Verse*, by Pastor D. A. Waite, 250 pages, hardback ($11+$5 S&H) fully indexed.
[ ] Send 1 Timothy--Preaching Verse by Verse, by Pastor D. A. Waite, 288 pages, hardback ($14+$5 S&H) fully indexed.
[ ] Send *Romans--Preaching Verse by Verse* by Pastor D. A. Waite 736 pp. Hardback ($25+$5 S&H) fully indexed
[ ] Send *Colossians & Philemon--Preaching Verse by Verse* by Pastor D. A. Waite ($12+$5 S&H) hardback, 240 pages
[ ] Send *Philippians--Preaching Verse by Verse* by Pastor D. A. Waite ($10+$5 S&H) hardback, 176 pages
[ ] Send *Ephesians--Preaching Verse by Verse* by Pastor D. A. Waite ($12+$5 S&H) hardback, 224 pages
[ ] Send *Galatians--Preaching Verse By Verse* by Pastor D. A. Waite ($13+$5 S&H) hardback, 216 pages
[ ] Send *First Peter--Preaching Verse By Verse* by Pastor D. A. Waite ($10+$5 S&H) hardback, 176 pages

Books on Bible Texts & Translations

[ ] Send *Defending the King James Bible* by DAW ($12+$5 S&H) A hardback book, indexed with study questions
[ ] Send *BJU's Errors on Bible Preservation* by Dr. D. A. Waite, 110 pages, paperback ($8+$4 S&H) fully indexed
[ ] Send *Fundamentalist Deception on Bible Preservation* by Dr. Waite, ($8+$4 S&H), paperback, fully indexed
[ ] Send *Fundamentalist MIS-INFORMATION on Bible Versions* by Dr. Waite ($7+$4 S&H) perfect bound, 136 pages

Send or Call Orders to:
THE BIBLE FOR TODAY
900 Park Ave., Collingswood, NJ 08108
Phone: 856-854-4452; FAX:--2464; Orders: 1-800 JOHN 10:9
E-Mail Orders: BFT@BibleForToday.org; Credit Cards OK

Order Blank (p. 3)

Name:_____

Address:_____

City & State:_____Zip:_____

Credit Card #:_____Expires:_____

More Books on Bible Texts & Translations

[ ] Send *GNOSTICISM: The Doctrinal Foundation of the New Bible Versions* By Janet Moser (241pp.$25+$7S&H)
[ ] Send *Fundamentalist Distortions on Bible Versions* by Dr.Waite ($7 3 S&H) A perfect bound book, 80 pages
[ ] Send *Fuzzy Facts From Fundamentalists* by Dr. D. A. Waite ($8.00 + $4.00) printed booklet
[ ] Send *Foes of the King James Bible Refuted* by DAW ($9 +$4 S&H) A perfect bound book, 164 pages in length
[ ] Send *Central Seminary Refuted on Bible Versions* by Dr. Waite ($10+$4 S&H) A perfect bound book, 184 pages
[ ] Send *The Case for the King James Bible* by DAW ($7 +$3 S&H) A perfect bound book, 112 pages in length
[ ] Send *Theological Heresies of Westcott and Hort* by Dr. D. A. Waite, ($7+$3 S&H) A printed booklet
[ ] Send *Westcott's Denial of Resurrection*, Dr. Waite ($4+$3)
[ ] Send *Four Reasons for Defending KJB* by DAW ($3+$3)
[ ] Send *Holes in the Holman Christian Standard Bible* by Dr. Waite ($4+$2 S&H) A printed booklet, 40 pages
[ ] Send *Contemporary Eng. Version Exposed*, DAW ($4+$2)
[ ] Send *NIV Inclusive Language Exposed* by DAW ($7+$3)
[ ] Send *24 Hours of KJB Seminar* (4 DVD's)by DAW($50.00)

Books By Dr. Jack Moorman

[ ] Send Manuscript Digest of the N.T. (721 pp.) By Dr. Jack Moorman, copy-machine bound ($50+$7 S&H)
[ ] *Early Manuscripts, Church Fathers, & the Authorized Version* by Dr. Jack Moorman, $20+$5 S&H. Hardback

Send or Call Orders to:
THE BIBLE FOR TODAY
900 Park Ave., Collingswood, NJ 08108
Phone: 856-854-4452; FAX:--2464; Orders: 1-800 JOHN 10:9
E-Mail Orders: BFT@BibleForToday.org; Credit Cards OK

Order Blank (p. 4)

Name:_____

Address:_____

City & State:_____ Zip:_____

Credit Card #:_____ Expires:_____

More Books By Dr. Jack Moorman

[ ] Send *Forever Settled--Bible Documents & History Survey* by Dr. Jack Moorman, $20+$5 S&H. Hardback book

[ ] Send *When the KJB Departs from the So-Called "Majority Text"* by Dr. Jack Moorman, $16+$5 S&H

[ ] Send *Missing in Modern Bibles--Nestle/Aland/NIV Errors* by Dr. Jack Moorman, $8+$4 S&H

[ ] Send *The Doctrinal Heart of the Bible--Removed from Modern Versions* by Dr. Jack Moorman, VCR, $15 +$4 S&H

[ ] Send *Modern Bibles--The Dark Secret* by Dr. Jack Moorman, $5+$3 S&H

[ ] Send *Samuel P. Tregelles--The Man Who Made the Critical Text Acceptable to Bible Believers* by Dr. Moorman ($3+$1)

[ ] Send *8,000 Differences Between TR & CT* by Dr. Jack Moorman [$20 + $5.00 S&H] a hardback book

[ ] Send *356 Doctrinal Errors in the NIV & Other Modern Versions*, 100-large-pages, $10.00+$6 S&H

Books By or About Dean Burgon

[ ] Send *The Revision Revised* by Dean Burgon ($25 + $5 S&H) A hardback book, 640 pages in length

[ ] Send *The Last 12 verses of Mark* by Dean Burgon ($15+$5 S&H) A hardback book 400 pages

[ ] Send *The Traditional Text* hardback by Burgon ($15+$5 S&H) A hardback book, 384 pages in length

[ ] Send *Causes of Corruption* by Burgon ($16+$5 S&H) A hardback book, 360 pages in length

Send or Call Orders to:
THE BIBLE FOR TODAY
900 Park Ave., Collingswood, NJ 08108
Phone: 856-854-4452; FAX:--2464; Orders: 1-800 JOHN 10:9
E-Mail Orders: BFT@BibleForToday.org; Credit Cards OK

Order Blank (p. 5)

Name:_____

Address:_____

City & State:_____ Zip:_____

Credit Card #:_____ Expires:_____

More Books By or About Dean Burgon
[ ] Send *Inspiration and Interpretation*, Dean Burgon ($25+$5 S&H) A hardback book, 610 pages in length
[ ] Send *Burgon's Warnings on Revision* by DAW ($7+$4 S&H) A perfect bound book, 120 pages in length
[ ] Send *Westcott & Hort's Greek Text & Theory Refuted by Burgon's Revision Revised--Summarized* by Dr. D. A. Waite ($7.00+$4 S&H), 120 pages, perfect bound
[ ] Send *Dean Burgon's Confidence in KJB* by DAW ($3+$3)
[ ] Send *Vindicating Mark 16:9-20* by Dr. Waite ($3+$3S&H)
[ ] Send *Summary of Traditional Text* by Dr. Waite ($4 +$2)
[ ] Send *Summary of Causes of Corruption*, DAW ($4+$2)
[ ] Send *Summary of Inspiration* by Dr. Waite ($4+$2 S&H)

More Books by Dr. D. A. Waite
[ ] Send *Making Marriage Melodious* by Pastor D. A. Waite ($7+$4 S&H), perfect bound, 112 pages

Books by D. A. Waite, Jr.
[ ] Send *Readability of A.V. (KJB)* by D. A. Waite, Jr. ($6+$3)
[ ] Send *4,114 Definitions from the Defined King James Bible* by D. A. Waite, Jr. ($7.00+$4.00 S&H)
[ ] Send *The Doctored New Testament* by D. A. Waite, Jr. ($25+$5 S&H) Greek MSS differences shown, hardback
[ ] Send *Defined King James Bible* lg. prt. leather ($40+$10)
[ ] Send *Defined King James Bible* med. leather $35+$8.50)

Send or Call Orders to:
THE BIBLE FOR TODAY
900 Park Ave., Collingswood, NJ 08108
Phone: 856-854-4452; FAX:--2464; Orders: 1-800 JOHN 10:9
E-Mail Orders: BFT@BibleForToday.org; Credit Cards OK

Order Blank (p. 6)

Name:_____

Address:_____

City & State:_____ Zip:_____

Credit Card #:_____ Expires:_____

Miscellaneous Authors

[ ] Send *Wycliffe Controversies* by Dr. H. D. Williams, perfect bound, 311 pages @ $20.00 + $5.00 S&H
[ ] Send *The Pure Words of God* by Dr. H. D. Williams, perfect bound ($15.00 + $5 S&H)
[ ] Send *Hearing the Voice of God* by Dr. H. D. Williams, perfect bound ($18.00 + $5.00 S&H)
[ ] Send *The Attack on the Canon of Scripture* by Dr. H. D. Williams, perfect bound ($15.00 + $4.00 S&H)
[ ] Send *Word-For-Word Translating of The Received Texts* by Dr. H. D. Williams, 288 pages, paperback ($10+$5 S&H).
[ ] Send *Guide to Textual Criticism* by Edward Miller ($11+$5 S&H) a hardback book
[ ] Send *Scrivener's Greek New Testament Underlying the King James Bible*, hardback, ($14 + $5 S&H)
[ ] Send *Scrivener's Annotated Greek New Testament*, by Dr. Frederick Scrivener: Hardback--($35+$5 S&H); Genuine Leather--($45+$5 S&H)
[ ] Send *Why Not the King James Bible?--An Answer to James White's KJVO Book* by Dr. K. D. DiVietro, $10+$5 S&H
[ ] Send Brochure #1: "Over *1000 Titles Defending the KJB/TR*" No Charge

Send or Call Orders to:
THE BIBLE FOR TODAY
900 Park Ave., Collingswood, NJ 08108
Phone: 856-854-4452; FAX:--2464; Orders: 1-800 JOHN 10:9
E-Mail Orders: BFT@BibleForToday.org; Credit Cards OK

The Defined
𝕶𝖎𝖓𝖌 𝕵𝖆𝖒𝖊𝖘 𝕭𝖎𝖇𝖑𝖊

UNCOMMON WORDS DEFINED ACCURATELY

I. Deluxe Genuine Leather

✦𝕷𝖆𝖗𝖌𝖊 𝕻𝖗𝖎𝖓𝖙--𝕭𝖑𝖆𝖈𝖐 𝖔𝖗 𝕭𝖚𝖗𝖌𝖚𝖓𝖉𝖞✦
1 for $40.00+$10.00 S&H
✦Case of 12 for $360.00✦
$30.00 each+$35 S&H

✦𝕸𝖊𝖉𝖎𝖚𝖒 𝕻𝖗𝖎𝖓𝖙--𝕭𝖑𝖆𝖈𝖐 𝖔𝖗 𝕭𝖚𝖗𝖌𝖚𝖓𝖉𝖞✦
1 for $35.00+$8.50 S&H
✦Case of 12 for $300.00✦
$25.00 each+$25 S&H

II. Deluxe Hardback Editions

1 for $20.00+$10.00 S&H (Large Print)
✦Case of 12 for $180.00✦
$15.00 each+$35 S&H (Large Print)
1 for $15.00+$7.50 S&H (Medium Print)
✦Case of 12 for $120.00✦
$10.00 each+$25 S&H (Medium Print)

Order Phone: 1-800-JOHN 10:9
CREDIT CARDS WELCOMED

www.ingramcontent.com/pod-product-compliance
Lightning Source LLC
Chambersburg PA
CBHW060533100426
42743CB00009B/1520